I

the SPIRITUAL SIDE of ARENTING

Introducing *the* SPIRITUAL SIDE *of* PARENTING

Raising tender kids in a tough world

RON CLARKSON

LION
PUBLISHING

Unless otherwise indicated, all Scripture references are from the *Holy Bible, New International Version®*. Copyright © 1973, 1978, 1984 by International Bible Society. Used by permission of Zondervan Publishing House. All rights reserved; other references are from *The Message* (TM). Copyright © 1993. Used by permission of NavPress Publishing House; the *Good News Bible*. Old Testament: (GNB) © American Bible Society 1966, 1971, 1976; *The Living Bible* (TLB), © 1971, Tyndale House Publishers, Wheaton, IL 60189. Used by permission.

Lion Publishing
A Division of Cook Communications,
4050 Lee Vance View,
Colorado Springs, Colorado 80918

Editors: Barb Williams; Brad Lewis
Design: Bill Gray
Cover Photo: James Barnett

1 2 3 4 5 6 7 8 9 10 Printing/Year 02 01 00 99 98

Dedication

To my precious wife, Ann, who has given me the gift of our five wonderful children

Ryan

April

Caitlin

Devon

Jordan

Contents

Acknowledgments

Books that didn't show up on my reference list:

Parenting with Love and Logic, by Foster Cline and Jim Fay.

Father Hungry, by Robert McGee, Vine Books.

Relief for Hurting Parents, Buddy Scott, Allon Publishing.

Kids Who Carry Our Pain, Dr. Robert Hemfelt and Dr. Paul Warren, Nelson.

My Father's Child, Lynda Elliot and Vicki Tanner, Wolgemuth and Hyatt.

Introduction

What's a Family For?

Have you ever heard the story about the woman who had five children. She lived in a small town that came under a tornado watch. She gathered her children and sent them to stay with relatives in a nearby town so they'd be safe. After the danger had passed, the children returned with a note that said, "Sending back the children. Next time, send the tornado instead!"

Have you ever felt like that in your parenting? "Help!" is the most appropriate four-letter word you can come up with! As a parent, you have the toughest job on earth. Parenting and the family are under attack. Many forces battle against you, and it's a tough job trying to build a strong family. While some have given up on the family and concluded that it's a thing of the past, I disagree!

Yes, the family is fragile. We need to fortify the foundation it is built on. But we can't give up on the family. We need a solid foundation so that we can withstand the storms of life.

Focusing on the spiritual side of parenting is the place to start building that foundation. Even a casual look at society today shows that people are hungry for "spirituality." From *Time* and *Newsweek* magazines running cover articles to document our interest in spirituality to best-selling books like *Chicken Soup for the*

Soul, people are looking for a connection with the spiritual dimension. This makes sense—we are created with a spiritual dimension. But how does this spiritual area of our lives affect our parenting? Many good books offer methodologies and techniques to help you negotiate the parenting maze. My hope is that this book will help you understand and practice the integration of spiritual principles into your parenting so it will be rewarding and effective.

You can find a good blueprint for the family by a master architect in the Book of Genesis. The family was God's idea in the first place. It was his institution. This blueprint reveals that God created Adam in a perfect environment. Adam had everything he could ever want. But God said, "It's not good to be alone." From the beginning of civilization, people were created for relationships. Today, we're still designed to function within relationships. Whether married or single, kids or no kids, we all need caring people to connect with. Men and women were not designed to be alone. The family was created and God pronounced it "good."

What's a family for? I heard someone say that he summed up "family" in a couple of words: bed and breakfast. For some, families are just an economic necessity. They get up in the morning, eat their bagels, have a cup of cappuccino, and head off to work. They may not even show up for dinner. They just need a place to nest at night. The next morning they get up and repeat the process all over again. Is this what a family is?

God says that the family is so much more than just a "bed and breakfast." If you are settling for that, then you and your family will come up short.

My hope is that this book will help you learn to celebrate and enjoy your children. I hope you see here the spiritual heart of a parent. I hope you'll want to count every day with your children as precious. I hope you'll see parenting as a wonderful place to develop great memories, that parenting will be much more than a task to accomplish. Above all, I hope you'll discover along the way some practical ways that you can instill in your children the values and morals you desire for them and the spiritual character that God created them to have.

—Ron Clarkson
Colorado Springs, Colorado

Chapter 1

To Parent or Not to Parent

Humor columnist Erma Bombeck once wrote, "I know I had three kids, but I wasn't sure why. I think maybe it was a 4-H experiment that got out of hand." As the father of five, I can relate to her statement. What makes parenting really scary is when your own children shake their heads in disbelief. In a moment of frustration one time, our third child, Caitlin, said, "Why did you and Mom have so many kids?"

My response was quick: "Would you have liked it better if we stopped after the second one?"

Did your parents feel this much pressure about parenting? When you think of your parents, what do you think of? You might say, "Wow, my mom deserved a purple heart for putting up with our family—the most selfless woman I've ever known."

Or you might beam and say, "Yeah, my dad was the greatest. He was my hero, always there for me. He's my role model."

Or you might have a neutral feeling about your parents. They were there, but not really in your life.

Or perhaps you would roll your eyes and say, "I remember Mom being too tired to do anything after working all day." Or, "All I remember about my dad was that he was never there."

Worse yet, right now you have a knot in your stomach. When you think of your father, you think of the emotional abuse you experienced or you cringe because of beatings you took. Or still worse, you are so hurt, so angry, because you were sexually abused.

When we talk about family and parenting, one thing is for sure: The subject is an emotional minefield. We're going to tread through that minefield and my hope is not to detonate any bombs. Instead I want to help us take a realistic passageway—not some idealistic blindfolded trek—into parenting.

Should You Be a Parent?

Of course, if you already have children, that's a stupid question. But I'd encourage you to keep reading, because even if you already have children, you might want to weigh just how prepared you are to raise them. If you don't have kids yet, read on for sure, because I believe valid reasons exist for why some people shouldn't have children. Maybe the most noble thing you can do is not have children or postpone having children for a season. The Prophet Isaiah said, "But the noble man makes noble plans, and by noble deeds he stands" (Isaiah 32:8).

Parenthood may not be for you. And the decision to bring children into the world should be accompanied by a whole deluge of prayer and sober thinking.

Why? What are some reasons *not* to have children?

Times Are More Perilous

Whether or not we want to admit it, the world is a much different place than it was a generation ago.

It doesn't take a social scientist or family expert to conclude that today's cultural climate is less conducive to raising a family.

When I was growing up twenty-five years ago, we sang "I Wanna Hold Your Hand." Today kids are singing, "Sex me...I want your sex." My mother would say, "I don't want you to be like that Eddie Haskell!" The worst thing Eddie Haskell did was give a "Dutch rub" to Beaver's head. Today we have rapists, murderers, mutilators. The teen magazines girls read when I was in high school talked about pimples and prom dresses. Now the same publications and new ones talk about contraception and cocaine. A recent ad by a formal wear rental store offered free condoms for anyone renting a tux from their store for prom.

No matter what the statistics say, you'll probably agree that the cultural climate is decreasingly favorable. Raising kids today will demand the most time and energy and greatest parenting skills of any generation yet.

Parents Are More Wounded

Record numbers of people of parenting age are coming out of divorced or broken homes. Record numbers are products of alcoholic homes or victims of emotional, physical, or sexual abuse.

One of the great societal ills is sexual abuse. While this problem isn't new, the number of incidents seems to be rising. Many people are discovering in their twenties and thirties that they were abused as children. The frightful increase in this problem—whether actually increasing or just increasing through more accurate reporting—doesn't provide much relief for us. Sexual abuse leaves a residual toxicity that can stick with us for life if we don't recognize it and work through it. It doesn't go away; it only resurfaces in other behaviors and other relationships later in life.

Victims of sexual abuse often believe damaging lies about themselves. "It's my fault. I deserved it. I could have prevented it." This lie piles on unwarranted guilt and shame. "Sexual involvement is the only way I can feel satisfied," or "I can protect myself from sexual hurt if I make myself unattractive," or "I hate my body and the way I look." These esteem bashers leave people who hobble through life with no or low self-esteem. When these people become parents, it's nearly impossible for them to raise kids who feel good about themselves.

Perhaps you experienced emotional abuse while growing up. Emotional abuse can come in the form of emotional neglect or emotional assault. Emotional neglect isn't necessarily a blatant act of aggression, but it's often the result of indifference or just not knowing any better. Your parents may have believed their responsibility was simply to provide a roof over your head, put food in your stomach, and give you the shirt on your back. But what about healthy cuddling and the affirmation and sense of belonging and acceptance necessary for any child? If you didn't receive this kind of support and environment, then it will probably show up as you struggle through relationships later in life.

Emotional assault usually comes in the form of a verbal attack on a child. It is usually packaged in the form of threats, embarrassment, belittling, or humiliation. Possibly you were made the scapegoat for your parents' divorce, or you were the brunt of every joke—the easy target. If you were on the receiving end of this type of treatment, you'll grow up with a distortion of who you really are. It affects your relationships down the road because they'll be flavored with distrust.

A look at the newspaper over this past Thanksgiving weekend was a grim reminder of the cycle of physical abuse. The picture on the front page showed a witness talking to police. The witness was pounding his clenched fist into his open hand—demonstrating for the police what he had seen his neighbor do to his own child. I'm not a prophet, but my guess would be that the arrested man probably was physically abused himself as a child. Statistics show this to be true: Parents who abuse their children were abused themselves. Physical abuse is a cycle, an important warning to those parents who may have suffered abuse as a child. That toxic anger needs to be identified and processed in the appropriate way.

If you suffered from physical, emotional, or sexual abuse, how can you break the cycle? How can you deal with the pain of your past so it doesn't infect your children? There's not an easy one, two, three answer. But the cycle can be broken. It begins with the element of honesty—being honest with your hurt, with the offense you received. Many people try to minimize the offense, believing it will minimize the pain. Be honest about the help you need to get in processing the pain. It might be through therapy or support groups. Processing your pain must also include forgiveness; otherwise the pain will be prolonged. The relief from the burden of bitterness and inward healing that occurs when you grow to forgive the offender is life-changing. Don't be afraid to seek help in this area for your own sake and for the sake of your children. (The resource listing at the end of this book contains the titles of helpful books and tools for dealing with healing from abuses.)

These traumas cause deep wounds. If the wounds aren't treated carefully and processed thoroughly, it can be toxic to all around you. These wounds can be toxic for your marriage relationship, and the poison often seeps through to children as well.

Jesus urged his followers to use judgment before beginning any project—and there's no reason to believe his words don't apply to having children and parenting. He said, "Suppose one of you wants to build a tower. Will he not first sit down and estimate the cost?" (Luke 14:28)

Before we begin to build a family, good judgment demands that we assess what it will take to build a family from the foundation up that will withstand the onslaught of cultural landslides and the destructive elements of our own wounds. Of course, our relationship with God allows us to tap the power and strength we need to withstand the negative elements of the culture and overcome the wounds caused by our past.

Still More Questions

It's difficult to change our culture and harder still to change the past. But when it comes to parenting, if you truly feel that with God's help, you can overcome concerns about the external and internal forces that impact families, I'd encourage you next to consider these three basic questions:

Question 1: What About My Marriage?

If you are married, you need to pay close attention to your marriage relationship. The health of your marriage directly influences your parenting. A healthy marriage is a loving relationship, not a limited partnership. It's a relationship that displays mutual respect and mutual submission. It's a relationship where trust flourishes. The depth of commitment and respect demonstrated by a mom and a dad to each other will be reflected in the emotional health and security of their children.

Perhaps you've seen the old cartoon showing the caveman holding a club in one hand and dragging his wife by the hair in the other. Though this is a caricature, it reveals a grain of truth many of us were exposed to in our upbringing. Dad was the boss, Mom the "hoss." Dad made the decisions, Mom and kids followed. And while Dad may not have been intentionally degrading, he never understood the mutual respect necessary to flesh out a strong loving relationship.

Or maybe your upbringing was the opposite—where the domineering mom made all the decisions and the dad's vocabulary consisted of those two nauseating words, "Yes, dear." Dad was the boss of the house and he had Mom's permission to say so!

Neither of these representations gets at the heart of what a loving relationship with mutual respect and mutual submission ought to look like. The Bible shatters some of our caricatures through its helpful teaching on relationships:

> Out of respect for Christ, be courteously reverent to one another. Wives, understand and support your husbands. The husband provides leadership to the wife the way Christ does to his church, not by domineering but by cherishing. (Ephesians 5:21-23, TM)

Respecting and submitting to one another means cooperation, not intellectual suicide. Collectively you use the wisdom and life experience God has given you to chart a course. The stronger your relationship and the more you demonstrate mutual respect, the stronger your marriage will stand in the storms of parenting.

Is your marriage relationship strong enough to bear the stress of raising children? A strong marriage relationship is where children see life work. They see values develop. They observe conflict resolution. They see faith worked out. A healthy marriage provides the platform for healthy, whole children to dive into life with vigor and gusto, not crawl through a meager existence with fear, distrust, paranoia, and low self-esteem.

A blunt word of caution: I don't believe it works to have children in order to strengthen your marriage. I've never seen this work in a marriage relationship, but I know of life stories where the opposite occurred. Many times I've listened to a tearful spouse say, "I thought if we had a baby, it would draw us closer together. It did for a while, but now we're right back where we were." Children don't make a marriage relationship stronger. Your marriage has to be strong enough to provide that platform to raise kids to wholeness and healthiness.

Question 2: What About My Wounds?

As I've mentioned, more and more people are wounded today. Due to the spiritual and moral decline of our culture, record numbers of parents are hurt, wounded, and tainted by their upbringing. What happens as a result? The brokenness can be passed from one generation to the next. Have both you and your spouse processed your personal "woundedness" to the point that it won't adversely affect your children? If not, you can pass a fractured legacy to your children.

You need to do something to stop the cycle of a fractured legacy, to pass on a baton that isn't broken. You may need to get counseling to deal with your anger, your alcoholism, your eating disorder, your dysfunctional behavior, your hurts, your wounds. You might need to find a support group. Certainly, you need to commit your life, your marriage, and your parenting to God.

One year, my wife, Ann, and our kids gave me a

bookmark for Father's Day. This verse is on the bookmark: "The righteous man leads a blameless life; blessed are his children after him" (Proverbs 20:7). I try to recognize and apply this truth every day. I resist asking God to make me successful or to give great wealth, prestige, or power. Instead, I remind myself that I need to be the kind of husband God wants me to be and the kind of father God wants me to be.

It's important to remember that our relationship with God can provide us with the strength we need to overcome even our deepest wounds. I remember the evening we had a phone call from a friend whose spouse had just walked out on the family. My son, Ryan, overheard some of the conversation and said, "How do you put up with this, Dad? How can you stand hearing all the pain and garbage people go through?"

I could have lied and said, "Well, Son, it's just because I'm an amazing individual." But I told him the truth. I told him that I believe God has the ability to take broken people and make them whole again. God has promised that he has the power and the desire to remake, reshape, and re-parent those who have been wounded. And it gives me joy and satisfaction to assure people that they have a heavenly parent who can heal the wounded, repair the broken, and give wholeness to those who have been torn apart.

Question 3: What About My Willingness to Sacrifice?

Finally, you need to weigh the cost of having and raising children. I'm not talking about the financial sacrifice—though it can be great. I'm talking about your willingness to give up self. Absentee fathers and divested mothers are not what kids need today. Parenting is not instant and kids are not microwavable to maturity. It takes time, effort, energy. It will cost you financially, yes. It might cost you career moves. It will cost you in your schedule. Are you ready to make these adjustments in your life? You should also ask these questions of yourself if you're thinking of *increasing* the number of children in your family.

If you already have children, you know that you seldom get a response of appreciation for all the sacrifices you make. Have you ever heard your kids say, "Hey, Mom, just noticed those stretch marks, and I want to say thanks for ruining your figure for me, carrying me around for nine months." Or have you ever heard, "Dad, just want to say thanks for driving that older car so I can wear designer jeans, eat three meals a day, and play in all those soccer tournaments."

Ann made the decision to postpone her formal education—for twenty years. Has she always enjoyed that decision? No. Have our children appreciated her decision? Seldom. But has she ever wavered in her willingness to pay the price for her kids? Never.

When you first gaze at that "special delivery package" from God called your child, you may be struck with an ominous feeling. This little entity is totally dependent upon you for everything—food, drink, clothing, shelter, comfort, security, affection, value system, and ideas about God. That's an amazing list of needs to accomplish in the short time we have our children. In

less than two decades, we're going to hand them over to a world that is mostly cold and calculated. The path for success in that world is forged by the job a parent does. How can we equip our children for that tough transition from dependence to independence, then to interdependence?

The challenge that lies ahead of a parent is enough to make us wonder, "What am I doing being a parent? I can't even get my kids to clean their rooms or eat their dinner, how can I prepare them for the real world? How can I raise kids who have their heads on straight and have a better-than-average chance to make it?"

If the Answer Is Yes . . .

All that said, let me tell you what I believe. Next to developing a relationship with God and your relationship with your spouse, raising your kids should be your highest priority. When you give your children their proper place and calculate the cost of raising them and making the necessary sacrifices, and when you follow God's plan for raising your kids, there's nothing in this world that will bring you greater joy. Yes, you will still face pain. You might overcome all the obstacles and do everything right, and your kids could still turn out with serious problems. But in spite of the pain and the difficulties, there's nothing greater than experiencing a family. There's nothing better than enjoying the community, the security, the safety, the shelter, and the fun of being in a family. Whatever the crises, as you watch your kids grow up and develop a strong self-esteem, as you observe them learn to love God and care for other peo-

ple, you will experience an unbelievable feeling of fulfillment. Nothing compares to the feeling of a family. Children are truly "a gift from the Lord" (Psalm 127:3, TLB).

If you've read this far and still want to have children (or another child), let me offer two other great reasons to have kids:

1. Children bring an intrinsic satisfaction to life.

What would my life be like without my family? Without a wife who doesn't let me get away with anything, yet loves me in spite of all my weirdness? Without children who make me happier, more fulfilled, than I ever thought I could be? I pray every day for my kids, that God will take care of them. And I also thank Him for what they mean to me, for the joy they bring.

I can't count the number of April and Caitlin's softball games I've been to in my parenting years. Once in a while, Ann and I would look at each other and say, "Well, we don't need to go to every game." Then we'd shake our heads and say, "Not a chance!" We didn't want to miss a single game. We love to see our kids compete! We love to see them be successful. We love the discipline they learn in athletics. And when they lose, make an error, or simply are down—we want to be there.

Children are a gift from God. They have awakened in me feelings I never knew I had, and I thank God for the privilege of parenting. I thank God when I lay down with my kids at night and they pray for people who don't have a home like ours or food on their tables. I thank God for my kids who want to give their pennies in Sunday School for a needy child. It's the greatest feeling in the world.

2. Children will impact tomorrow.

I also thank God that someday my children will be involved in a positive way to impact this world. I don't need to hope that one of my children will become President, find a cure for cancer, or is the next Michael Jordan before he or she can make a difference. If my kids understand the importance of character over charisma, they'll make an impact with their lives. If they invest their lives instead of spending them, then they'll make an impact. And if they communicate to their kids and their circles of influence that every person has intrinsic value and really matters, then they'll positively influence their own generation and generations to come.

The greatest thing I can do for society is to produce healthy, whole children who understand God's love and forgiveness in their own lives and seek to share that with others.

While Ann and I made the choice to have children, it doesn't mean everyone should. If you're already in the midst of parenting, you need to be the healthiest parents you can be so you can pass on a legacy that is whole. Make the most of every day, every hour, every minute. After you've read this chapter, take a look through your photo albums. Kids grow up awfully fast. But if you commit to making the most of every moment, you'll reap the joy of these precious gifts God has entrusted to you.

Chapter 2

Raising Tender Kids in a Tough World

The past few years, there's been a lot of talk about the family. From talk shows to politics, there's been a call for a return to the family. It seems that nearly everyone thinks the family is the solution to society's problems. While the news reports that crime, violence, and gangs are all at epidemic proportions, people are calling for a return to the family as "the only solution."

Even our own President has said, "The hope of our society is in the family."

When I hear these statements, I get concerned—even afraid. If the hope of our society is in the family, we could be in big trouble, because the traditional family has been disintegrating for roughly the last three decades.

Times are changing! The divorce rate increased by

279 percent from 1970 to 1992.[1] The number of children living with a divorced parent jumped 352 percent from 1960 to 1990.[2] Even though children of divorced parents are more committed to seeing their marriages work better than their parents', they are actually more likely to divorce themselves.[3]

I believe some major myths have been launched into society and gained momentum over the past few decades. These myths have landed in our hearts and have been injected into our parenting processes.

Myth 1: Kids Are Resilient

This first myth is scary because it's not simply a misunderstanding. It's a myth that may prove fatal. I bought into this myth when I began parenting. I even taught it to other parents. But once I corrected this myth, it made a dramatic impact on my parenting.

My wife was a widow when we wed. Before we got married, I had some serious thinking to do about becoming an instant dad. I would enter marriage with a ready-made family! I debated whether or not I was ready to take on this task. I read books and sought counsel. Do you know what I was usually told? "Kids are resilient. They bounce back pretty well."

So I went into my marriage thinking, "These kids are resilient, they'll bounce back." It wasn't until about four or five years into my marriage that I learned my kids are not as resilient or as tough as I thought they were.

The truth is my kids were very fragile. I also found out I'm not as tough as I thought I was. When I was growing up, being tough meant burying things. You know, "Come on, pull yourself up by your boot straps. Nothing hurts us. We're tough." But what we've really learned to do is to bury things.

If we buy into the myth that our kids are resilient, do you know what we teach them? To bury things as well.

Many of us have bought into the thinking that the family can withstand a constant barrage of attacks because the family is tough. We think that to improve its resiliency, we can reconfigure the family. We can drift away from God and his plan for the family and expect it to stay intact.

But it's a lie. It's a fatal myth. We've got to replace the myth with the truth that the family is fragile. Jesus Christ says this:

> People were bringing little children to Jesus to have him touch them, but the disciples rebuked them. When Jesus saw this, he was indignant. He said to them, "Let the little children come to me, and do not hinder them, for the kingdom of God belongs to such as these." (Mark 10:13-14)

Jesus knew that kids were not resilient. We like to think kids are like Nerf balls. You can squeeze a Nerf ball, you can sit on it, you can stomp on it, but it always bounces back to the same round shape. Kids are more like eggs—fragile, delicate, and requiring careful handling. If you shake up a child's world, you end up with scrambled eggs. If you put the child through all kinds of heat and hot water, you come up with a hard-boiled kid.

One of the most traumatic events in the life of a child is divorce. In the past few decades, the laws have changed to make divorce easy.

Research substantiates the claim that children are and will be adversely affected. According to psychologist Urie Bronfenbrenner of Cornell University, "Controlling for factors such as low income, children growing up in [single parent] households are at greater risk for experiencing a variety of behavioral and educational problems, including extremes of hyperactivity and withdrawal; lack of attentiveness in the classroom; difficulty in deferring gratification; impaired academic achievement; school misbehavior; absenteeism; dropping out; involvement in socially alienated peer groups, and the so-called 'teenage syndromes' of behaviors that tend to hang together—smoking, drinking, early and frequent sexual experience, and in more extreme cases, drugs, suicide, vandalism, violence, and criminal acts."[4]

As children of divorced parents grow into adulthood, there can be additional consequences. Dr. Nicholas Zill found that adult children (18–22 years old) from divorced families were twice as likely to exhibit problems than those who came from intact families, even after controlling for demographic and socioeconomic differences.[5]

I know many people who have gone through the pain of divorce. I certainly hope that no judgmental attitude or spirit comes through here. What I'm trying to say is this. If you've been through divorce, I know that you have hurt and pain. You need to know that no matter what you have been through, you matter to God. You need to understand that there is nothing you've done that puts you out of God's reach.

The Bible says that God hates divorce, but you will not find anywhere in the Bible that God hates divorced people. He loves divorced people. He loves the families that are struggling through these issues. And he is the only way you are going to get through this situation. What God is opposed to is those who treat marriage in a casual fashion, someone who decides, "I'll bail out now and cut my losses early—regardless of the hell it raises in my family."

God hates divorce because of the wreckage left in families—the casualties. God has always known that the family isn't as tough as we think it is. It is fragile. Think of how fragile kids are. What does it take to break the heart of your little girl? Your little boy? It doesn't take a whole lot, does it? What does it take to crush the spirit of a child? Or your spouse? It doesn't take a lot, does it? All it takes is one moment of selfish insensitivity to dash the dreams or disseminate the trust of your family members. And when you do, you short-circuit your ability to give and receive love.

What about the hurt caused our families by addictive behaviors? We're usually smart enough to figure out that if we're struggling, our kids won't escape the fallout. Even our best attempts to cover up, clean up, or clam up won't leave our children unmarked. The effects of addictive behavior are passed on to those we love.

And what about absenteeism? Mom or Dad is off to work, out of town, gone on business, staying late—and the list goes on. Like never before, our society is raising a generation of children who have been relegated to latchkey settings or secondary caregivers. Kids aren't resilient. They need present and active, alive and well parents who are painfully aware of possible residual effects their children may experience based on the life-choices parents make.

Here's some help for overcoming Myth #1: None of us were raised in perfect homes, and none of us are perfect parents. I try to live in a constant awareness of how my choices, my decisions, and my words affect my kids. I get frustrated with my kids more than I want to and more than I probably should. Sometimes I express it with some thoughtfulness and control. Other times . . . well, I really foul up. I get angry. I say things I shouldn't. Or I give my kids the silent treatment. None of these are appropriate and each one affects my children. I can pretend they don't, but they do.

But if I swallow my pride, get face-to-face with my kids, and apologize for my actions, I find that whatever damage I caused dissipates quickly. I've never had one of my kids ever say, "Stick it in your ear, Dad. I'm going to make you sweat this one out." Instead, the forgiveness is swift, unconditional, and appreciated.

There is nothing in your past that you have done that is unforgivable. Maybe you've messed up in your parenting through absenteeism. Maybe you've not been there emotionally for your kids. Maybe you've hurt them deeply through a failed marriage. Maybe your anger has been heaped onto your kids. Maybe you've believed they possess enough resiliency to make it. Most of the time, their resiliency isn't enough.

You need to forgive yourself and receive forgiveness from God and others. You can face the wrong choices you've made—the same ones thousands of others have failed at as well—and get it right this time. The great thing about your kids is that they will give you a second chance—a second, or a third, or a fourth!

Myth 2: NutraSweet Is as Good as Sugar!

The second myth that we have bought into is more subtle, but perhaps at least as dangerous to the well-being of the family. This myth claims that parental substitutes are as effective at child rearing as parents are.

Over the past several decades, the financial and cultural pressures on the family directed mothers back into the workforce at a record pace. Child-care facilities have multiplied, yet we haven't stopped to ask the question, "Is it really healthy and advantageous to decide to have children and then hand them off to a child caregiver in our attempt to work so we can keep up the lifestyle we have and pay off the debt we have accrued. Should we be willing to make that exchange?"

Note that I'm not intending to bash working moms here. I'm certainly aware of the pressures families face and the economic realities that force parents to make some choices they don't particularly like. I'm talking instead about the message our society has tried to send that says we shouldn't worry about who cares for our kids, as long as they have "appropriate adult supervision." While I know that many families feel trapped in this cycle, and I know that there are many qualified caregivers watching children, I think the myth is simply untrue. Parents cannot relegate the nurturing and care needed by their children to a detached third party, no matter how gifted or qualified. There is no substitute for active parental presence.

Each word in this phrase is important. It's not simply the presence of parents; it is active parental presence. This is essential for a healthy family. As I mentioned earlier, the divorce rate has increased by 279 percent from 1970 to 1992 and the number of children living with a divorced parent climbed 352 percent between the years 1960 and 1990. Add to these the fact that the number of children living in single parent homes has increased 108 percent in the last two decades. In 1970, 12 percent of children under the age of 18 were being raised by one parent. In 1980, that number increased to 20 percent. In 1990, it was as high as 25 percent. Out of wedlock births have soared by 400 percent since 1960.[6] Today, 1 in 4 children live in single-parent homes. On any given night 40 percent of children go to bed without a father in the home. (The latter statistic doesn't assume that there's been a divorce in the home! Just because you are divorced doesn't mean you aren't there as a parent, and just because you are *not* divorced doesn't guarantee that you *are* present as a parent.)

My younger kids have taught me to be there, to pay attention to them. Sometimes, my youngest will grab my face and turn it toward his face so we are eyeball to eyeball when he is talking to me and say, "Daddy, I'm here." We need to be there for our children—with our hearts, our eyes.

A few years back I was mentored by an individual who was very successful in his circle. I learned a lot about business from him. But I also learned something else—he was willing to pay a price for the success he desired. I was single then. But as I watched his family life, I thought to myself, "Something isn't right with this picture." His idea of spending time with his children was for them to come to the office where he'd throw a Frisbee in the parking lot with them. Even as a single person, that bothered me. He'd bought into the myth that because his kids were young, they were resilient. He believed his wife's job was to care for the kids, and his job was to get his organization up and growing. And it grew. It grew to the point where Mom also joined the staff of the organization. That created a personal child-care crisis in their family. So this family moved Grandma and Grandpa to "live in" with the family and take care of the kids. Noble? Yes. Necessary? Well, when I saw that, I made a commitment that this personal example would be one mentoring pattern I'd live without.

Active parental presence is essential for a healthy family. Don't misunderstand me. I'm not saying that you should never put your children in day care, or never take them to a baby-sitter. You need to get away from your kids sometimes to develop your relationship with your spouse. If you're single, you need breaks from your kids to be better equipped to handle them alone. But that's not the same as entrusting your children to someone else to raise them.

Parental substitutes are not as effective as loving,

nurturing, actively present parents.

Of course, overcoming Myth #2 is much easier said than done. For example, who isn't under financial pressure today? It's tough to make it through the hits of inflation without having to work long, extra hours if you're a single parent or having both parents work. How can you make the best of a not-so-good situation?

1. Keep tabs on the time.

Child care is essential for families with working spouses. But one less project, one less sale, one less optional business trip is well worth the time exchange with your children.

2. Keep tabs on the budget.

One problem with our society is the desire to spend right up to and then a little over what's budgeted. Any increase in income or windfall goes to buy another pleasure, not reduce overhead. If your budget is never under control it may be time to see a financial counselor. Be on guard if you find yourself spending your potential family time trying to make more money to provide things for your family. You might make more money and provide more things, but you won't be around to see your family enjoy any of it! They'd rather have you than things.

3. Find a "kid-friendly" job.

Find a job or arrange your schedule to maximize the time you spend with your kids. This may mean less money or less prestige. It may mean forfeiting advancement in your company. But you know the exchange value, you know which investment will really pay the dividends!

With our third child heading off to college soon, my wife has had to go to work full time. When searching the marketplace she had several different opportunities, yet she selected one that would best fit the life of our kids. I've also had to make adjustments in my schedule to accommodate her move into the marketplace so that our kids could benefit.

4. Take a break.

If you find yourself away from your kids longer than you want to be during the workday or you have no choice but for your child to be in day care longer than you would like, at least take a break. Stop by the caregiver's location and "do lunch" with your child. If your kids are in school, do lunch with them at school once in a while.

My own schedule runs long and hard, working Sundays as well as Monday through Friday. But I've made it a priority to "put in my schedule" special events like field trips, breakfasts at McDonald's, and school musicals. The breaks allow me to keep a healthy pace at work, yet often make my kids' day as I focus on them.

Myth 3: Value-Free Rearing

You might recognize yourself in this myth. Many parents who are now raising children were raised in the 1960s and 1970s in a value-free (or at least value-unimportant or value-different) environment. Much of our culture and our educational system disposed of time-tested and proven child-rearing practices. These gave way to the philosophy which warned of the dangers of "indoctrination" of children in values, ethics, and faith.

On the surface, of course, this reasoning has some appeal. It urges parents to keep from "cramming values down the throats" of their kids. "If you force-feed them, they'll just throw it up." The idea was that the kids would never really assimilate the values for their own. There is some truth to this. I've seen it fleshed out in many situations where people have crammed religion or a particular set of cultural expectations down the throats of their children, and it did more harm than good.

But the line of reasoning goes on like this: "Wait until your kids grow old enough to make those kind of choices and decisions on their own. Given time, they'll be able to strain out the unnecessary waste and concoct answers to their own values and spiritual dilemmas."

I'm going to be blunt again. If children are "a gift from God," then as parents can we really wash our hands of the responsibility to build, develop, and form spiritual and character values in the lives of our children? Do any of us really believe this has worked? Are our kids better when it comes to values today? I believe we have robbed our children of a moral compass to help them navigate the dilemmas and tough issues of life. Values and morality cannot develop in a vacuum. The development of a moral compass and the ability of our children to develop a sense of right and wrong pours out of years of *proactive and persistent* value teaching.

Again, the Bible offers these words to parents:

> Love the Lord your God with all your heart and with all your soul and with all your strength. These commandments that I give you today are to be upon your hearts. Impress them on your children. Talk about them when you sit at home and when you walk along the road, when you lie down and when you get up. (Deuteronomy 6:5-7)

For thousands of years, the Bible has taught that parents are accountable for influencing the values of their children. If this is God's Word, should we guess that it's any less true today? God has given parents a teaching responsibility, a modeling responsibility, and an instilling responsibility. If we rob children of the moral teaching they need, we rob them of critical skills they need to fend off the avalanche of corruption that will bury them. And if you raise your kids with no concept of God—the God who loves them and cares for them and values them—then you're doing them a disservice. If kids are raised not knowing about the heavenly Father who loves them and will stick by them—no matter what happens to Mom and Dad—then you deprive them of an irreplaceable segment of reality that they critically need to make it day-to-day in a tough world.

To accomplish what is expected, you just need to be present. Spend as much time with your kids as you can. You have them for a short season. Make sure your children know you love them. Tell them again and again and again. They never tire of hearing you say it.

I have a master's degree in theology from a famous graduate institution. But when I lie down with my kids at night, I don't read from the Greek text of the Bible or from St. Augustine. I don't teach them about elaborate theology. I tell them how special they are, how much I love them. I tell them about their heavenly Father who loves them even more than I do.

Don't drown your children in content. Marinate them in the love of God, and they will absorb his values as they grow through life.

1. Statistical Abstract of the United States; 1993. (1994) U.S. Bureau of the Census (113th edition), Washington, D.C.

2. "Families First." (1993) Report on the National Commission on America's Urban Families, John Ashcroft, Chairman, Washington, D.C.

3. Norval D. Glenn (1991), "The Recent Trend in Marital Success in the United States," *Journal of Marriage and Family*, 53:261–270.

4. Urie Bronfenbrenner, "Discovering What Families Can Do," in *Rebuilding the Nest: A New Commitment to the American Family*, David Blankenborn, Steve Bayme, and Jean Bethke Elshtain, eds. (Milwaukee: Family Service Agenda, 1990).

5. Nicholas Zill, Donna Morrison, and Mary Jo Coiro. (1993) "Long-Term Effects of Parental Divorce on Parent-Child Relationships, Adjustment and Achievements in Young Adulthood," *Journal of Family Psychology*, 7:1, p. 91.

6. "Families First." (1993) Report on the National Commission on America's Urban Families, John Ashcroft, Chairman, Washington, D.C.

Chapter 3

Signs of Family Strength

Years ago, when my wife and I were dating, she was a quiet, calm, laid-back, patient person. As we spent time together, I began to realize that I really liked this woman—maybe I even loved her.

Between the two of us, I was the one who mutual friends would have described as "living life on the edge." Then one day Ann took this Iowa farm boy to the San Diego Bay for sailing. I thought it would be fun to sail with this woman I was growing to love. We'd skim around in the water, see some beautiful scenery together, then call it a day.

Surprise! When this quiet, calm, wonderful woman got into her eighteen-foot Hobie Cat catamaran, she suddenly turned into a wild, thrill-seeking, hull-flying maniac! She wasn't content to just sail peacefully along.

She wasn't even happy trying to keep one hull in the water. Her object was to get the tip of the sail as close to the water as possible!

The longer we sailed, the more I began to wonder. She was smiling from ear to ear while I was ready to throw up from motion sickness. I asked myself: Is this *normal*?

Life can be pretty unstable if we don't know what normal is. A lot of us wander through life trying to figure out what normal means when applied to our families. What does a normal family look like? What are the signs and gauges we can use to measure the strength of our family?

Years ago, when we lived in Chicago, we planned a trip to see relatives in Iowa in the middle of winter. One of the girls had a swim meet, so we weren't able to leave until late at night. If you've ever driven from Chicago to Des Moines, you know there's not much in between!

When we took off at midnight, the temperature was 18 degrees below zero and the snow was blowing hard. Somewhere in the middle of this midnight snowstorm, I glanced down at the dash of our van. The temperature gauge was climbing. Though I'm mechanically challenged, I was pretty sure this wasn't a good sign.

Within minutes the gauge moved out of the green zone of safety into the red zone. When my male instinct kicked in, I took the usual first course of action: I thumped the gauge with my index finger. Surprisingly, that didn't work. So here we were, out in the middle of nowhere in a snowstorm, Ann, our five kids, and me in the van. I shut off the engine and pulled over to the side of the road. We huddled under blankets and waited twenty minutes to start the van again. Then we drove until the warning gauge started to edge into the red zone. I thumped the gauge again, then pulled over and shut off the engine. I kept this up for an hour—starting and stopping—until the engine finally died for good.

Fortunately, we were picked up by a snowplow. He didn't have enough room for all of us so he called another snowplow. We landed at the Illinois Highway Commission where we were safe.

When I ignored the warnings and tried to keep driving, I should have known what was eventually going to happen. The gauges were telling me to take some action—any action but to keep driving! The end result was that the engine was completely shot. The shell of the van looked great, but it wasn't going anywhere.

This can happen to families too. A warning light comes on over here with your spouse, an alarm sounds over there with one of your children. But you just keep going. And then . . .

What are some gauges that might help you measure the health of your family? Perhaps identifying these gauges will encourage you that you're doing some good things in your family. But maybe a warning light will go on, and you'll be alerted to unhealthy patterns in your family of origin or in the family you now lead.

A Healthy Family Affirms Individuality

God, in his sense of humor, decides to put people into families who are completely different from one another. Chances are you're married to a spouse who is opposite from you in a number of ways. While similarities pulled you together in the first place, the opposites are what you found interesting about each other and why you pursued your relationship.

Each of us is created with individuality. If you have two children, it soon becomes obvious how different they are. When the second one hits the crib, you know he's completely different from the first child. One is the "good baby" who sleeps all the time. The other one, the "difficult baby," gets up at 4 or 5 in the morning and throws off your whole body clock.

The problem intensifies when these babies mature. That "good baby" becomes a teenager who continues to sleep around the clock. You can't blast him out of bed with dynamite. Now he becomes a "difficult baby." And that "difficult baby" who got you out of bed is the one who doesn't wear out the snooze bar on his alarm. They're so opposite that you wonder how these two kids ended up in the same family.

By the time you put together a marriage and throw a couple of children into the mix, you probably look at one another in your family and conclude: "You are so weird! You must be from a different planet because what you want is so different from what I want." But God breaks through our thick skulls with some powerful verses. King David reminds us that God shaped us first inside, then out. God's workmanship is wonderfully complex and marvelous:

> For you created my inmost being; you knit me together in my mother's womb. I

> praise you because I am fearfully and wonderfully made; your works are wonderful, I know that full well. (Psalm 139: 13-14)

God has wired us differently, not wrongly. You need to be able to recognize the differences in your family and celebrate that uniqueness. Not only will this enhance relationships within your family, but as you go outside in society you'll be better equipped to relate to others and their differences.

In healthy families there are no black sheep. There are no carbon copy kids of Mom and Dad, no sculpted children. Will our kids be able to look back on a home where they felt free to be themselves? In chapter 7, we'll look more at how you can build your child's self-esteem and provide some practical ways to encourage individuality.

A Healthy Family Affirms Value

Another gauge of a healthy family is a willingness to affirm value. Perhaps one of the greatest signs of valuing your family is recognizing the need to get counsel to deal with the tough issues of family life. Proverbs 13:10 reminds us that "pride only breeds quarrels, but wisdom is found in those who take advice." Our family is much richer because of the counseling we've received to help us process our difficult issues.

Valuing your family means that each individual is recognized as vital to the family. Every person is created in God's image and placed by Him into your family.

Valuing means vowing never to abuse, shame, or intimidate one another.

You don't have to look hard in local papers to find cases where families have not made the vow to value each other. Recently, I read of a woman whose children were taken from her because she abused them. The prosecutor stood up and said, "Someone has to start speaking up for the child and the unborn child and not worry so much about the needs of the mother."

We need to make a commitment that we are never going to even get close to abusive treatment of family members, whether emotional, physical, or sexual. The most pain-ridden people in the world today are the souls of damaged children who looked to their parents for love and nurturing but received abuse instead.

Perhaps as you read this, you feel incredible pain. A sinking feeling is beginning to overtake you right now because you endured abuse in your family of origin. You looked to your parents for support and hugs and kisses. Instead you received emotional or verbal abuse or slaps and kicks. You may have been sexually violated and invaded by an adult. You know firsthand the long-term scars of this kind of damage.

It's important for you to seek professional counseling to deal with these issues, and to ensure that as the formerly abused, you don't become the abuser. Will you vow to affirm the value of each member of your family, and never abuse, intimidate, or shame them? With the help of a skilled counselor, and the strength and power and love of God, you can do it

A Healthy Family Communicates Love

The Bible gives us incredible pictures of God's love for us. A verse in 1 John describes the marvelous love the Father has extended to us:

> How great is the love the Father has lavished on us, that we should be called children of God! (1 John 3:1)

This provides an excellent illustration of the way we should operate in our families. In the same way your heavenly Father lavishes his incredible love upon you, so you should do to your children.

In the Sermon on the Mount, Jesus teaches us a similar truth. He reminds us that even earthly fathers give incredible gifts and lavish love onto their families. Incredible love is the kind that amazes onlookers. It's the kind of love that makes a college student come home and scratch his head and say, "Wow! I can't believe what Mom and Dad put up with. I really miss being home."

Incredible love is the kind described to me this week by a friend who told me of his mother's death. "That woman was amazing," he said. "She raised five of us kids as a single mom and left a permanent impact on me and my whole extended family."

Incredible love is the kind a new dad feels as he stares at his son in the delivery room. He doesn't say, "These are your tax-free years, son. Make the most of them!" He looks at that newborn baby and says, "I love you! I'm making a vow to display unconditional love to you. I don't care how well you perform in sports or academics, or if you never walk on the moon. I'm committed to love you with no strings attached."

> Love is patient, love is kind. It does not envy, it does not boast, it is not proud. It is not rude, it is not self-seeking, it is not easily angered, it keeps no record of wrongs. Love does not delight in evil but rejoices with the truth. It always protects, always trusts, always hopes, always perseveres. Love never fails. (1 Corinthians 13:4-8)

A Healthy Family Communicates Grace

Communication ranks at the top of all the lists of trademarks of healthy families. The Bible gives great insight as to how we are to communicate:

> Instead, speaking the truth in love, we will in all things grow up into him. . . . Do not let any unwholesome talk come out of your mouths, but only what is helpful for building others up according to their needs, that it may benefit those who listen. (Ephesians 4:15, 29)

Healthy interaction between parents and children is at an all-time low. The television set is on seven hours a day on the average. Mothers spend twelve to fifteen minutes of undivided attention each day with their children, and fathers spend only two to four minutes a day.

Note the common thread connecting TV viewing, sleeping, and working. None of them invites interaction between members of a family. Thus it becomes critical that family members intentionally commit time to one another.

One of the top frustrations kids have is they don't get to communicate with Mom and Dad. If Dad is in the home, perhaps he travels too much. Mom is so maxed-out that her children don't know who to turn to when they need to connect. We may try cell phones, pagers, and e-mail messages. But these don't fill the void kids have to connect with parents on a deep level. And kids don't always know how to articulate this need. So while our kids fill their minds with values from TV or their peers, we wonder, "Why is their ability to make good decisions so haywire?"

Mom and Dad need to set the pace in the family for healthy truth-telling and communication of grace. If our communication pattern is unhealthy or nonexistent, our children will grow up with a void. If Mom and Dad can't communicate truthfully and gracefully with one another, our children most likely won't learn how to communicate either.

We need to expend the time and energy necessary to create windows of opportunity for connecting with our kids. Maybe your family needs to rediscover the lost art of having dinner together in the evenings. That doesn't mean sitting down and buying a vowel from Vanna White while you're eating! Turn off the TV! Focus on your family's schedules. What are their priorities and problems? Who are their friends? What's happening in school? What kind of homework help do they need? What are they struggling with? What things do they enjoy? If you can't answer these basic questions about your children, you've got some work to do.

Seize opportunities to teach values. Don't just sit back and complain about what your kids are learning in school. Get involved in the process. Set up date nights with your kids. When my son was home from college recently, we spent a lot of "hang-out" time together. We went to the gym, played basketball, and went to the movies. But at one point, I said, "Let's go to lunch, because we need to talk about the issues that have tripped you up this past semester. How are you going to get over those hurdles?"

How about the communication time spent with your kids? Do you find it tough to make conversation unless it's about something like sports or fashion? Try these ideas to jump-start communication with your children that's beyond the polite and superficial.

1. Evening news/newspaper.

The news of the day provides an excellent springboard for the discussion of values. This is particularly true of world events where the paradigm is different than the Western mind. At our home, for instance, we've had great discussions about political leaders in the Middle East. How does their faith affect their actions? Why do some religions teach their followers to treat others with such hatred?

2. Holidays.

Holidays are great for establishing traditions, but they're also an important communicator of grace when we give up some of our discretionary time to do a community service project. It might be a soup kitchen, a Salvation Army project, a provision for a needy family. Each Christmas we get involved with Project Angel Tree—a program that provides Christmas gifts to children of those who are incarcerated.

3. Report Cards.

"You've got to be kidding! Grade reports bring nothing but stress into our house—if they even make it to our house!" Hold on! Report cards can be a great tool of communication—more than just the obvious. They can be used to launch into discussions and action plans regarding work ethic, honesty, and goal-setting, in addition to a great example of the principle of cause and effect.

A Healthy Family Teaches Respect

When I hear how a lot of kids talk to their parents and other adults, I realize we have an epidemic of disrespect in our country. Teachers are intensely frustrated by the disrespect in their classrooms. They're tired of being verbally abused and threatened. I recently spoke with a policeman who told me, "I'm not afraid of the criminal who will shoot me in the back. I'm worried about the teenager who just for grins will blow me away right in my face!"

Disrespect isn't just a problem in this country. Apparently, it's a worldwide epidemic. I talked with a man who had spent time in Rwanda making a documentary. He told me:

> Our crew had to take turns on the camera. As long as we were looking through the lens, we could become immune to what was happening around us. It was as if we were just watching from a distance on TV. But when we had to step away from the camera and tune in to the murder and genocide all around us, we couldn't believe the devaluing of humanity we witnessed. How sad that much of this country is churched! But there is an intense vacuum in their value system.

One of those "teachable moments" to reinforce respect for life occurred in our home as we talked about Chinese orphanages. We'd seen a documentary on TV, and my wife was ready to adopt a couple hundred kids. "They could live in the basement!" she insisted. Of course, the rest of the family pointed out that we already have five kids and "we don't need any more in this house!" But we continued talking about the overpopulation in China and the killing of baby girls. Our son, Jordan, six at the time, took this in. His prayers that night weren't for Mommy, Daddy, or Chester our cat. They were for the kids in China. Though it was tough on him, I thank God for the chance we had to see our son develop this sensitivity because he saw firsthand the devaluing of human life.

We need to take a hard look at what we're teaching about respect when we pass on racial or ethnic or sexual slurs. Do our "harmless" comments devalue individuals made in the image of God? We would do well to remember the words of that children's song: "Jesus loves the little children, all the children of the world; red and yellow, black and white, they are precious in his sight."

Another teachable moment in our home has come through our oldest son's friendship with Billy. Billy, Ryan's best friend, is African-American. I quizzed our youngest two one day. "What do you notice that's different about Billy?" I asked. Their first response? "Well, he's really good at Nintendo." After a while they finally acknowledged, "Oh, yeah, his skin's a different color." But to them it was no big deal.

My heart breaks when I hear racial slurs. God reminds us, "You have never looked into the eye of an individual who didn't matter to me. And if I valued these people enough to die for them, don't you think they deserve to be treated with dignity and respect?"

Let's remember the admonition in Galatians:

> Let us not become weary in doing good, for at the proper time we will reap a harvest if we do not give up. Therefore, as we have opportunity, let us do good to all people. (Galatians 6:9-10)

Of course, there are many situations in addition to race, where your modeling of respect will be an essential teachable moment for your children. How about that "radar detector" in your car? Think about the message you might be sending your children: "It's OK to break the law, just take whatever steps are necessary to not get caught." Respect for the law and those who enforce it is something all parents should feel obligated to teach. Positive comments about the police and family trips to visit a police or fire station are great ways to teach that respect.

How about respect for teachers? Contrary to conventional wisdom, I don't think a lot of the problems in our educational system are the fault of administrators or teachers. Instead, the strength of our schools rises and falls on parental involvement and interaction. You can complain about the schools, but do it after you've become involved in your child's class, supporting the teacher and the school. When you're involved, you have the right to make evaluations and criticisms. This teaches your child respect for education, as well as the proper way to evoke change.

And what about respect for other family members? Home is supposed to be a place where children can draw security and significance. Unfortunately, the home sometimes instead becomes a place where a child is demeaned, picked on, ridiculed, or singled out. This is confusing and often damaging. My kids get into fights. They get upset, mad, mean, and nasty. We want them to say what they feel, but we closely monitor comments that are degrading and demeaning. We've decided that demeaning comments are not how they feel; these comments are just what they feel like saying. There's a difference. If my son says, "I'm ticked that my sister took my car and left the gas tank empty. I think that's pretty inconsiderate," he's expressing how he feels. But if he says, "That dog face sister desecrated my car with her scuzzy body and then, like the lazy blimp she is, left my gas tank empty," he's crossing over the "respect" line.

Regarding respect for other adults: Do you remember when you were young you learned to call other adults Mr. Smith or Mrs. Jones. Even family friends might have been "Aunt" or "Uncle." Today, respect for elders has seeped from our culture. I was at my daughters' swim meet and we were sitting in the front row bleachers with some other parents. The mom I was next to was cheering her daughter in a close race. A couple of high schoolers walked in and stood right in front of her. She tapped them on the back and said, "Could you move please?" One of the high schoolers replied with expletives I can't record in a family book. I got pretty amped up. I stood up (I'm 6 foot, 3 inches and 200 pounds), leaned down into his face, and told him what I thought about his disrespectful attitude. Then I reported him to the principal!

Respect for other people is a rudimentary life principle we must demonstrate for our children to learn. It's important because it becomes a watershed issue for all of life's interaction.

A Healthy Family Teaches Responsibility

In addition to teaching respect, we need to teach our children how to live responsibly. This won't come easily, because all around us we see people not taking responsibility for their actions. Politicians skirt telling the truth, then pass the buck to someone else. Religious people do things in the name of God, then blame their behavior on others. Criminals and gang members commit inconceivable crimes, then point the finger of blame on anyone or anything but themselves.

It's popular to be a "victim." Many people in our

society believe that we are owed particular rights and privileges. But healthy families remind their children that we aren't just "takers," but we must learn to give as well—and often the give and take won't balance in our favor.

Sometimes it's easier to look the other way than it is to tell the truth and set limits in our families. But if you do this, you'll find that it's the irresponsible family members who end up controlling your household. It could be an overpowering in-law, a child who is acting out, or an abusive spouse. You need the courage to stand up to them and say, "You will not be allowed to manipulate this family. You will not make this house a miserable place to live."

I'm not speaking from a vacuum on this "tough love" issue. I'm speaking from the depth of my heart. Ann and I had to go through this (see chapter 10). The toughest thing you might ever have to say to a family member is, "You will not be allowed to put this family through hell anymore. We're drawing the line. You have a choice to make about what you're going to do." That's tough love. That's teaching responsibility.

Our children need to learn to keep their commitments, to do what they say they will do. When they give their word, they will follow through. They need to grow up to be adults who will pay their bills, who will complete tasks.

My children hear a phrase over and over from me: "No 80-percent jobs." They know that we expect them to do a 100-percent job in completing their chores. And they hold me responsible. Sometimes when we're doing dishes, I'll hand a glass or pan I've washed over to my kids to dry and they'll pass it back with a reminder, "That's an 80-percent job there, Dad!"

Teaching responsibility is tougher with some kids than with others. My youngest daughter, Devon, loves to do a job well the first time. But when my son, Jordan, walks into his room, he sees an "explosion" and can't figure out how it all got there! He falls on the floor and cries, "This is too much to do, Daddy. I can't!" And he dares to ignore the flow charts and project diagrams I've prepared to make the task of room cleaning more efficient and manageable! Of course, it's too easy to get distracted with the Legos or other toys that now landscape his room. He takes a lot more work than his sister because of the way he's wired. It's a longer process with him, and we patiently walk through the process with him and keep nudging him toward taking more responsibility for his room.

Every day you have opportunities to teach small, yet tremendous character lessons. How well are you doing at instilling a sense of responsibility in your children? Most parents realize that when you have high schoolers, they'd rather die than ride the school bus anymore. This issue, which could be a source of contention and aggravation for Ann and me, has become a great opportunity for our kids to develop responsibility. As most parents know, every other kid in the world owns a car but them. Simple solution—if our kids want a car, they pay for it! If they want to drive, they pay for the insurance! It's really been a workable deal with them. They have the privilege and the freedom, but they realize that freedom has a price—there are no free rides!

Healthy Families Share Play Times

My childhood is rich with memories of backyard ball games, sledding, campouts, wrestling matches, and waterskiing. I remember my dad playing a gorilla game. He'd jam a banana in his mouth, mess up his hair, and come at us like King Kong. We'd scream, laugh, and growl back all at the same time.

We often take the fun out of parenting by being too serious. Healthy doses of fun, laughter, and "cutting up" keep a family strong. It's part of our job as parents to provide an atmosphere of fun for our kids. Laughter and humor provide some great building blocks.

Laughter and humor are part of building a child's self-esteem. During one of our visits at Grandpa Lew's in Iowa, Jordan was taking a ride on Grandpa's shoulders. The view from the top of Grandpa's shoulders is pretty awesome from what I remember, but Jordan was more taken with Grandpa's haircut. When Jordan asked Grandpa where he got his haircut, the reply was that Grandma cut his hair. As he checked out the sizable bald spot on Grandpa's head, Jordan asked, "Why does she shave a big hole in the middle of your hair?"

Grandpa about died laughing and Jordan felt that he was a pretty funny guy. When Grandpa told everyone he ran into about that story, Jordan felt even funnier!

Humor is also a good way to develop cooperation with your kids. Yes, I know they should do something "just because I said so," but it's OK to lace your instructions with some humor. It not only lightens the atmosphere, but it teaches your children some social skills as well. They can learn to joke with people, and they can learn to ease tension and solicit cooperation through the use of humor.

Kids are kids for just a short time. It's a shame that some of them grow up missing out on the "fun" that makes life just a little better. Take advantage of the time you have with your kids to have fun, enjoy life, and create humorous memories.

I'm learning how much kids love play times. Baseball in the cul-de-sac, sledding, wrestling, storytelling, waterskiing, snow skiing—these will create some of the most significant memories our children will have. We need to spend a lot less time at the office, a lot less time lecturing and disciplining them, and more time playing with them.

Healthy Families Share Traditions

Another significant area healthy families share is traditions and rituals. They provide our children with a sense of security, consistency, and predictability. Your kids might not ever say to you, "Thank you for implementing these traditions." But as the years pass, you'll discover the value and significance of these rituals.

Over the years we've established some great family traditions. Birthdays are celebrated with friends who get invited to parties, but we always have special dinners with just our family to celebrate the honored person. We have a Valentine's Day dinner every year. We have a 4th of July party—open to any of our kids' friends who want to come. We go camping in the mountains every summer—a family vacation that has created some of our greatest memories. We have an annual Halloween chili feast before we go "trick-or-treating." We spend Thanksgiving doing the same thing every year—holding our annual "Turkey Bowl" flag football game. Our daughter was away at college in Hawaii this year, yet called us for a month ahead of time complaining that she couldn't be with us for Thanksgiving. I thought the beach and snorkeling might take away some of her pain, but what she wanted was "the tradition."

Christmas brings with it our tradition of decorating gingerbread men and our Christmas tree on the same night. During Ryan's first year of college, he called home and told us how much he was missing this tradition. Ann shipped his gingerbread men overnight so he could still be part of it!

Healthy families believe in traditions. Traditions say to all of us, "We did this in the past and we're doing it right now. We're going to do this year after year after year." This provides a secret power of continuity and security in our homes.

What you leave your children in your will really doesn't make a difference. You might amass a fortune, and you might set up trust funds. You might help them buy a house once they're on their own. But what your kids really need—even when they're out on their own—is you. You and your legacy. Build a treasure into them instead of amassing a fortune away from them. Instill in them a trust of you and your integrity, not a trust of currency. And don't be so concerned with gifting your children with earnest money for a house after they've grown. Instead be earnest to gift them with a home while they grow.

Chapter 4

The Time of Your Life!

young boy was a terror in the house. Finally, out of desperation, his mother bought him a bike.

His dad asked, "Do you think the bike will help?"

His mom replied, "No, but at least it will spread it out a little bit."

Sometimes we're just so exhausted with everything going on in our lives that when it comes to our kids, we have no energy left. We think, *Maybe if I just keep them occupied, then I can get some rest.* Of course, then we feel guilty for not spending more time with them.

OK, then. *If I keep them occupied with something I need to do, then I'll be spending time with them and getting my task done.* You've probably tried this. It rarely works for long.

I've been there. I've believed that if I can just keep

my kids occupied, it will fulfill the need they have to spend time with me.

Nice try. But what we forget is that children spell love: T-I-M-E.

A Valuable Product

Time is one of the most valued commodities in our lives today. But don't you sometimes feel like Gumby in the hands of a toddler? All those people and pressures pulling and stretching us for our time. The competition for our time is intense and demanding. None of the time-saving mechanisms—fax, cell phones, e-mail, overnight delivery—have relieved our schedule at all! They haven't bought us another single minute. They have only freed up more minutes or hours to increase our productivity.

How important is it to spend time with your family? The first step is to evaluate what's taking time away from your kids. If you find yourself saying, "I have to provide for them," you might need to examine the true motive behind your words. Perhaps the words of warning Jesus spoke provide a good measurement:

> Watch out! Be on your guard against all kinds of greed; a man's life does not consist in the abundance of his possessions. (Luke 12:15)

If these words strike just a twinge of guilt in you, it's OK. Use them to make a little movement in your life. Use the letters in the word *time* to help you.

T—Take the Time

Take a break—particularly from your work—to spend with your family. I can't really tell you how. I can only tell you that you need to do it. Figure it out somehow, because the alternative is unacceptable. Whether you're working inside or outside the home—or both—you need to re-prioritize your life and make a commitment to "take the time."

One step toward figuring out how is to see if this description fits you. Are you trading more and more of your time to be able to buy or purchase more material goods? If so, think about this: The more time you spend, the less time you have to enjoy. None of us has more than twenty-four hours in a day, so there's a point of diminishing return.

There's more to life than 8 to 5—and it's not making your workday 7 to 6. There's more to life than the money market and savings accounts. You're worth far more than your checking account balance. I hope you believe that your children are! Too many of us confuse our net worth with our self-worth.

Your relationship with God and your family are a higher priority than gaining financial or vocational advancement. Think about it: When you stand before God someday, do you think he'll ask you how much money you made? Or how many promotions you received? I think he'll ask you, "How did you do with the people I entrusted to you—your children?" What answer will you be able to give?

If you don't believe your family is your highest priority, then apparently you've fallen for the mother of all sound bites: When it comes to spending time with your family, it's not the *quantity* of time, but the *quality* of time. Now that sounds profound. In fact, I used to believe that and practice it. The truth is, this kind of thinking is faulty. I'll be even bolder; it's a weak excuse.

"It's not the quantity, but the quality." You know, we won't accept that dichotomy anywhere else in our lives. I've spent a lot of time at the dentist recently. I'm a wimp when it comes to the dentist, so I say clearly each time, "You're giving me novocaine, right?" What if his response was, "You bet, but I'm only going to give you 1 cc instead of the normal 10 ccs"?

"What are you talking about?" I'd scream.

And what if he then said, "Oh, don't worry, it's *quality* novocaine. It's the best novocaine on the pharmaceutical market." That's great. It may be quality novocaine, but it still wouldn't be enough to get the job done.

Face it, you simply can't spend ten action-packed minutes with your kids at the end of the day to make up for the fact you haven't spent time with them all day. We need to spend *quantity* time, not just *quality* time with our family. We need to spend large amounts of time with our children and our families because quality moments occur spontaneously *during* the quantity of moments.

Spending quantity time, a lot of time together, means spending time that is relaxed and enjoyable. These times don't just happen. You have to make the time. You have to *plan* it.

I know it's not easy. I'm a pastor. My days are filled

and many of my evenings could be too. When you throw in other family member's schedules, life can be like a zoo.

That reminds me of a story about the Hong Kong zoo that I read in *Newsweek*. As the zoo grew in popularity and was more heavily visited by human observers, the animals grew noticeably fatigued, unhealthy, and more edgy and testy with each other. The concerned zoo officials finally decided that perhaps the animals needed a day off. So they began closing the gates to the public one day a week. The animals showed some improvement, but there was still some fighting and sickness. So the zoo started closing two days every week. The results were amazing! The health and playfulness of the animals was quickly restored.

If we just don't have the energy to spend quantity time with our families, maybe we should try closing the zoo. If the behavior of our children isn't what we would like it to be, maybe we need to close the zoo another day. Maybe the pressure thrown at your family is more than they can tolerate. Hang up the closed sign, draw the shades, take the phone off the hook, and spend some time—a lot of it—with each other!

I—Initiate a Plan

Make plans for your family. Make a conscious decision to cut back on other areas of your schedule. Give up at least a little piece of the rat race—it may be costing you your family. Comedian Lily Tomlin once said that no matter who wins the rat race, it's still a rat!

Do you realize there are an awful lot of rats in your race? So you're not going to win. (And if you do, you'll still be a rat!) So, give it up! Set in motion a plan to make necessary changes in your life.

Your children are the most important entities you can build your life into. You must successfully build your family first. Not your business. Not even your ministry. Before God, you are responsible to your children—to love them, to spend time with them, and to build character qualities into them first. Your coworkers, your friends, your church, your clients must all follow your children.

It doesn't just happen. You have to make it happen. Plan for it to happen. If you don't intentionally make time with your family, it won't happen. It never does.

I know that none of us have truckloads of discretionary time. Do we just sit around and say, "Gee, I have nothing to do. Maybe I'll just go out and clean the garage." Not in this life! We say, "Saturday morning, after T-ball and before soccer, I have two hours to get the garage clean." It's the same with exercise, recreation, and spiritual development. It's true in all areas of life. It's especially true with our children! Initiate a plan; it won't "just happen."

Grab your calendar. Now make a concentrated, irrevocable, conscious decision to make the time necessary with your family. Plan it. Protect it. Treat your family times like they were an appointment with the President. Plan time that you refuse to sacrifice and spend it with your family on a regular basis. How much? Every minute of every day that you can find! If necessary, do some open-heart surgery on yourself. Use a scalpel to cut away some of the scheduling fat surrounding your heart for your family.

Now comes the hard part! Ha! The times you plan need to be exciting, creative, and challenging to the initiative of your children. Don't just sit around and watch TV. The average American family spends 7 hours and 12 minutes per day watching television.[1] Let's assume that we are pretty un-American and only watch 3 hours of TV per day. At less than half the national average, we will still watch more than 60,000 hours of TV in our lives. That's more than seven years of TV programming in your life at under one-half the national average. That's about 10 percent of your life!

And remember that television is not only competing for your time, it's competing for your values. Many of the shows send messages that conflict with the values you work hard at instilling into your children. In addition, sitting around the TV damages the creativity of children and hinders interaction and communication within the family. There's no feedback or sharing of lives when we get stuck in the couch potato mode.

I'm not saying, "never watch TV." We have a TV and a VCR in our home, but their use is regulated and monitored. We even use the TV occasionally for family time. We like to rent a good movie, make a fire, break out the pillows and blankets, and have a slumber party. But we have to watch out for TV as an "easy out." Parents need to seriously consider what is quality time together and what is baby-sitting or laziness. Guard against the lack of initiative to plan and initiate creative, fun, family-time activities. Refer to the book list *An Introduction to Family Nights* (ChariotVictor Publishing).

Do you take vacations with your family? Let me ask you another question: Does your briefcase join you on your family vacations? How about your cell phone? Your laptop computer? Getting a little too close to the truth? Don't rob your family of the time they need and deserve. Guard your vacation time and plan to leave distractions behind.

Our family once took a great ski vacation to Bryan Head, Utah. It was a great time teaching the kids to ski. Ann was pregnant with our fourth child, Devon, so she couldn't ski. Everything was just perfect, so I thought. Before starting my day, I would call back to my office in San Diego. I was sneaky enough to make those calls when Ann wasn't around. Funny thing, when we returned at night, there would be a message from my office. It seemed OK for me to call the office staff, but it really bothered me to have our office staff join us via phone conference on our vacation. It was a powerful lesson.

The following summer, we made plans to visit relatives and old friends for our family vacation. Then we decided to change our plans—a decision for our immediate family's benefit. We knew that our vacation would be robbed as we tried to visit every aunt, uncle, niece, nephew, cousin, in-law, and outlaw. Extended family is great, but sometimes everyone wants a piece of you. Instead, we spent our family vacation alone on a lake in the Ozarks. And I'd learned my lesson. My briefcase and calls back to the office weren't a part of it.

Vacations don't need to be expensive or extensive. But they do need to be intentional. Our kids still remember the summer vacation when we camped our way back to the East Coast. The hassles of setting up camp, no electricity for blow-dryers and curling irons, cleaning fire char off pots and pans, and sleeping on the ground were soon forgotten. But the memory of the family time was indelibly marked in the minds of our five children.

M—Make Some Memories

When you reach the end of your life and your children gather at your bedside, what will they identify as the happiest moments of their lives? "Gee, Dad, do you remember that time that we watched 'Wheel of Fortune' together?" No, it's the time you got them their first bike. (In my case, it was also the first time they heard Dad swear because of the idiot who wrote the assembly instructions.) It's the time you took your daughter out on a date to a special restaurant. The time you went skiing in the mountains or boating on the lake. It was the hours you spent in front of the fire telling knock-knock jokes or around the campfire telling spooky stories. It was staying up all night to help with the school project just to see the look of pride in your children's eyes when they marched into class the next day.

What are you doing right now to build the memories you'd like your children to have? Memories imprint children for a lifetime. It's not just special things that can create memories. Even the ritual of doing things over and over gives memories a "forever" quality. It's never too late to start a family tradition.

A few years ago, Ann and I decided to start our own traditions at holiday time. It wasn't as easy as it sounds. We already had the tradition of visiting relatives at Christmastime. You know the game plan—trying to divide yourself and your family equally between all your relatives and by the end of Christmas you feel as though you've been sliced and diced and made into fancy fries. So, we decided to spend Christmas at our home, with our tree, with our immediate family. The goal was to establish new traditions for our own home.

Our kids still look forward to some of the traditions we've established. Our daughter came home from her first year of college just for our family Valentine's Day dinner. We've had these simple traditions for years. There were even times during their adolescence that my kids complained about the traditions. But one by one, they're beginning to see the value those memories have.

Sometimes we're so busy giving our kids what we didn't have that we don't take time to give them what we do have. What we do have might just be some great memories and good traditions that will take time and effort to build.

Children are precious and they deserve the best of our time and energy—not our leftovers.

Remember when Jesus blessed the children who were brought to him after the disciples tried to stop people? Jesus had a special place in his heart for kids. They were significant and precious to him. His disciples didn't seem to share his feelings. After all, they were quite busy learning to be his disciples, keeping up with their jobs. But Jesus rebuked them for their inconsiderate attitude. Jesus touched children and held them in his arms. He blessed them, and I think each of those children could look into his eyes and comprehend how much he cared for them.

In the same way, your children need to know that their presence in your daily life is important. You need to communicate to them how glad you are to see them at the end of your workday and their school day. Sometimes I wonder if we're so anxious to make sure they've done their chores and homework that we forget to let them know we care about them.

E—Eyes, Listen with Your Eyes

Kids don't want you to listen with just your ears, they want you to listen with your eyes. I can recall more than one occasion when I was parked in front of a Bulls' game, eyes and heart glued to the TV. My wife has told me that I probably didn't even realize my children were in the same room with me, let alone hear whatever they were talking about.

I'm adept at juggling multiple balls. My job demands it and my personality enjoys it. But I've learned that paying attention to what my kids are trying to say is not a ball to be juggled. It's a time that demands my focus and undivided attention. Sure, there are times when it's impossible to do that—like when a mom has a screaming sibling with dirty diapers in one hand and the computer mouse in the other as she attempts to reconcile the bank statement. How do you spend the necessary time listening to your kids?

Here are three principles that will serve you well if you can put them to work:

1. Remove distractions.

There must be a regular and consistent—even designated—time when you remove distractions from your immediate surroundings and focus on what your child needs to tell you. Removing distractions does not mean hitting the mute button on the TV remote. It means turning off the TV and other distractions, going up to a room or out on the porch—somewhere you won't be interrupted and dialogue can flow freely.

It also doesn't mean taking your child to a movie. There's nothing wrong with that, but it's not a place where dialogue can flow between the two of you. Instead, take your child on a date. This is what I've tried with my daughters. We dress up, go to a restaurant of their choice, and just spend the time talking.

2. Be waiting to listen to them.

I have a real problem trying to do this. I like to finish tasks. As a result, I often tell my waiting kids, "I'll be with you as soon as I finish this." They wait for a while, but I get so engrossed in what I'm doing that they get tired of waiting and leave. Worse yet is if I'm so focused on my task that I don't see them walk off.

Wouldn't it be nice if our children found us waiting to talk to them? "Hey, when you get off the phone, I want to spend some time with you." What if every day after school, when they walk in from soccer practice or band rehearsal, we were sitting on the couch waiting to listen? Or what if you called your daughter from work and said, "Are you going to be home for a while? I want to leave early and take you to get a yogurt."

Creating these opportunities does unbelievable things for your child's self-esteem: they feel valued, they feel important, and they believe you really want to listen to them. It also puts another strand in the braided rope of your relationship with your son or daughter.

3. Tell them what you heard.

At night, while you're tucking your kids in, kissing them good night, or saying a prayer with them, be sure to tell them something that you remember from your conversations. "Honey, I think bubble gum yogurt might become my favorite too." Or, "Hey, buddy, I'm glad you like Bobby for your best friend. I think that's a great choice." Or, "I'll be praying for you about which college you want to go to. I think you'll know for sure by the time you graduate." These restatements affirm to your child that you listened and that you cared enough to remember.

Our children need to sense that we want to spend time with them, that it's not just an obligation. They need to know that we're devoted to them and that we'll tell them and show them we love them by spending time with them. Children who know they are loved feel good about themselves. And they're better able to handle any difficulty life throws at them.

An anonymous children's poem says:

> I hate to sound selfish,
> like everything's mine,
> but please don't get mad
> when I ask for your time.

The amount of time you spend with your family is an indicator of the commitment you have to them. Ask yourself these questions:

• The waking hours of each day have about a thousand minutes—how many are spent with your family?

• There are 168 hours in a week—how many do you spend with your family?

• The average life is 30,000 days (80 years). We sleep a third of that, leaving 20,000 days. How many of those days are spent with our family?

Time is like oxygen: A certain amount is necessary to sustain life before damage takes place.

I heard this true story of a busy man in Los Angeles. His wife asked him if he had remembered their son's birthday. After squirming, he finally asked what their son wanted for a present. His wife told him that their son had said, "Well, if Dad is going to be around, I want a football so we can play catch. But if it's going to be like it has been, then get me a soccer ball so I can play by myself."

Ouch! How would your kids answer?

1. George Gerbner. (1994) "Television Violence: The Art of Asking the Wrong Question," *The World & I*, July, 389.

Chapter 5

Who Needs the Family, Anyway?

You remember the old expression, "I feel like I've been hit by a freight train"? When I come home at night, that's just how my wife often feels. Five kids—two boys and three girls—dog, cat, laundry, dishes, husband. . . .

Parents who have kids in the toddler stage know the freight train feeling well. Toddlers can crush things, flush things, spill things, kill things, eat things, and beat things—all with a smile on their faces! Someone has said, "When God made Adam from the dust of the ground, he did a good job. Then when toddlers came along, God added electricity."

Toddlers aren't the only ones who can drive you crazy. No matter what stage of life your kids are in—whether preadolescence, adolescence, postadolescence, early adulthood—your family can cause chaos. The chaos is a given. The question is: How do you remain committed to the family in the midst of all this chaos?

The Family Research Council, a coalition of psychologists, educators, and government officials, has studied strong families. They listed five things that were the top ingredients in strong families. The number one thing? Commitment. Love didn't even make the top five ingredients, but commitment did.

What is commitment? Commitment is *love in action.* Commitment is a cornerstone for the family, a foundation strong families are built on. It's the attitude of "I'm in this thing for the long haul." Families need to know that something in life is secure. They need to see and feel the glue of commitment that will hold them together.

A while back I counseled a couple planning to get married. Their backgrounds were quite diverse. Robert's parents were well into their second decade of marriage. Yet Robert's fiancée, Christa, had a story that sad movies are made of. Her dad had taken off when she was just a year old—after he'd tried to kill her twice. Her mom had given up after several marriages and now changes men like they're long distance companies.

I encouraged this couple to talk things out, to consider how their backgrounds would tie into their own marriage. They needed to learn the old adage, "Love is blind, and marriage is an eye-opener!" I looked them straight in the eye and said, "Unless you are committed to marriage, unless you commit that divorce is not an option, I refuse to marry you. I want to be a part of your wedding, but there is a deep understanding of commitment that you both need to arrive at."

They didn't think counseling was necessary and called me later to tell me someone else was performing their marriage. I wish I could tell you that I was wrong and that they lived happily ever after. But soon after their first baby was born, they divorced and headed into an ugly custody battle.

If you don't take commitment seriously, your path will lead to pain and devastation—or mediocre survival at best. One of the most beautiful pictures of commitment to the family is found in the biblical story of Joseph. Joseph ran the gamut of emotions when it came to feelings about his family. But he possessed an immutable commitment. He was hated by some in his family, loved by others. He was betrayed by his brothers. They even plotted to murder him! But the thing that held him strong, that ultimately saved his own life as well as the lives of his family, was his commitment.

Joseph started out on the wrong foot. He was "daddy's boy" and his dad didn't try to hide it. His brothers despised him for it. They hated him so much that they wanted to kill him. But when a shred of sibling compassion took over, they decided to sell him instead.

The slave traders who bought Joseph from his brothers ultimately took him off to Egypt. His brothers went back and told their dad, "He's been killed by an animal." Joseph went to Egypt and rose to the top, becoming second in command in all of Egypt—second only to Pharaoh.

Many years later when a great famine hit the land,

Joseph's brothers showed up to apply for welfare in Egypt. They came in front of their brother, now the ruler. They didn't have a clue they were standing in front of their little brother until he identified himself. Surprise! Joseph made all the decisions and held the power of life and death in his hand. Joseph's family was scared to death, but Joseph calmed their fears by saying, "Am I in the place of God? No, that job is filled. I want to show love and compassion to you."

Now Joseph could have been possessed with animosity, hurt, rejection, and sibling rivalry. But his ultimate commitment to his family was displayed through his love in action.

How can you develop that kind of commitment to your family? First, you need to understand that commitment will cost you. It won't be easy, but it is accessible. Commitment costs, but it also P-A-Y-S. Here are some ways you can grow in commitment.

P—Prioritize Your Life

Of course, the idea of prioritizing your commitments isn't new. We hear it all the time. But its familiarity doesn't diminish its importance. Unless we prioritize, our lives are left totally to chance. Do you want the major choices of your life left to chance?

Here are two vastly different life stories of men who have prioritized their lives. One is Orel Hershiser, world-famous pitcher, who played in the 1997 World Series. In an interview he related, "Money is only part of the equation for success. My attorney has suggested that every time I want to assess my Major League career I ask myself: 'Am I still married? Are my children happy? Does my family know me?' If I can answer 'yes' to all of these questions, then I'm having a great career."[1]

The other is Pete Rose, formerly of the Cincinnati Reds. While he was known as "Mr. Hustle" by sports fans, he's known in a less endearing way by family members. In an interview, his daughter said, "He's the world's worst father. I will never understand why he never had any time for us. We didn't expect anything from him, except just to like us."[2]

Pete Rose was interviewed the day after his daughter's article in the paper. When asked about his daughter's comments, he said, "I don't know what she's complaining about. I bought her a new Mercedes last week."[3]

Then interviewers spoke with his son, Pete Rose II. He recounted how he'd been prevented from telephoning his dad. "Even if I wanted to call him, I don't have his number. I have to call his agent and he tells my dad I want to talk to him."[4]

What a difference of priorities! Each choice leads in a different direction. If you want to build a strong family, you have to begin with appropriate priorities.

Establish a Relationship with God

The foundation for priorities in your life should be a personal relationship with God. Remember when Joseph revealed to his brothers who he was? When they feared him, he said, "Am I in the place of God?" He had a clear understanding of the importance of a relationship with God. It allowed him to be committed to his family to such a degree that he would forgive them unconditionally and provide for them.

Maybe you're frustrated in your family life. Maybe you need to get your foundational priority—your relationship with God—in order. This relationship is important for the next commitment.

Make an Unconditional Commitment to Your Spouse

Judging by a lot of TV programs, many movies, and popular magazine articles, it's hard to imagine that you can be normal in today's society and actually want to, plan on, and enjoy being faithful to your spouse. How many relationships portrayed on the screen and in print are actually healthy, dynamic, married couples? Former NFL all-pro superstar Roger Staubach—Super Bowl champion quarterback for the Dallas Cowboys—stated it quite well in an interview on ESPN. The interviewer was comparing his lifestyle with the playboy-like lifestyle of former New York Jets quarterback Joe Namath. After some frustrating questions, Staubach finally said to the interviewer, "I like sex as much as Joe Namath. I just like it with one woman—my wife."

Talking about fidelity in marriage used to be a noble thing. Today, though, people tend to neglect what you have to say because they presume you're approaching the subject from a close-minded, old-fashioned, out-of-touch, puritanistic paradigm. But when it comes to the impact upon your children, fidelity to your spouse demands your attention.

Your children derive their sense of security within your family from observing the stability of their mom and dad's relationship. How strong is your commitment to your spouse?

Most marriage counselors and professionals feel that the breakdown in the family today begins with marital infidelity. We idealize highly romantic relationships. We see it on daytime television and in romance novels. It's easy to begin believing the message that if life isn't perfect here, you can find a better situation somewhere else. But these media don't accurately portray the true picture. They don't expose the deep hurt caused by betrayal. There's very little in this world that is more painful than a spouse suffering the pain of infidelity. It's not just the sense of betrayal or the breaking of trust, but the act itself becomes life-threatening. An unfaithful spouse returning home to be sexually involved with his or her married partner now brings the potential risk of a sexually transmitted disease. In today's world, that's like playing Russian roulette with your spouse.

The pain and brokenness that accompanies infidelity cuts to the emotional core of the offended party as well. The ultimate physical display of intimacy—a sexual relationship—has now become a shared group activity. What was once a promise to express this kind of love to "you and you alone" becomes a shattered dream.

And what about the children? Running through their minds are thoughts like this, "If Dad can't keep a promise to Mom, what's going to keep him from breaking one to me?" Or, "If Mom really isn't that committed to Dad, who she says she loves most, then what's left for me?" Infidelity rocks the security of the entire family. It derails the stability that children need to feel at home. That's certainly not attractive. This unattractiveness is the part you don't see in the movies where unbridled romance is exonerated.

Now I'm all for romantic relationships. Without sexual intimacy and oneness, marriage is an empty shell. Romantic intimacy is something God created and considers to be good. But we all know that emotions are unstable. They fluctuate. In strong marriages, there are times you feel close to one another and other times when you don't even like each other. Ann has let me know on more than one occasion that she loves me, "But today I don't like you very much. You're being kind of a jerk!"

It's like the woman who put the ad in the paper, "Lost: husband and dog who left on fishing trip. Reward for dog."

But what will get you through the highs and lows of the marriage? What ingredient will carry you through those times when you love each other but don't really like each other? It's the commitment of your will, the commitment to say, "I'll stick to this marriage."

Demonstrate a Commitment to Your Family

When I come home from work, where I've expended a lot of energy and creativity, I don't walk in the door and say, "Gee, I can't wait to put in some good, hard work into my relationships here at home." I usually hope that there is some semblance of peace and order. I hope one of the kids isn't tied up and held hostage by another. I hope each child's homework is done. I hope my wife doesn't want to talk about her day, because I'm in no mood to tell her about mine!

It takes energy and creativity to be committed to your family. The success of any group, whether a sports team, management team, task force, or family, depends on the commitment of each person to the group. This kind of commitment needs to be an everyday commodity. What gets families through crises is the day-to-day assurance that they can count on each other. Instead of independence, families can count on interdependence. Instead of being a Lone Ranger, you're part of a posse. Instead of feeling like a kamikaze pilot, you're part of an entire air force.

So what are our three most critical commitments? First to God, then to our spouses, then to our families. Note that work doesn't even make the top three! That's a big struggle for me, because I love to work. I love the challenges and sense of fulfillment that the marketplace brings. At one point in my life—not long after Ann and I were married—I loved work so much so that soon I was stuck in the same cycle so many people find themselves in. I was working a job in San Diego I loved, the organization was extremely successful, and I was spending more and more time away from home. I enjoyed the rush of my job! But as I worked more, I also became more and more desensitized to my own core values. It's not that hard to get upside down when things are going well—or even when they aren't!

After a heated exchange with my wife about my seventy-plus hours a week, I was forced to step back and look at what was going on. I liked the results of my work, but the process was making me sacrifice everything I really valued—my wife, my kids, and my integrity. That night I made the decision to leave the organization. I worked out a plan to give notice and switch jobs within three months, and that ultimately transpired.

I look back on that decision as a turning point in my entire life, and I've thanked God that I received the wake-up call before it had further negative impact on my family. I'm not sure if it was a smart move financially or if Chicago's winters were a good trade for San Diego. But I've never regretted the decision, nor have the benefits of the decision stopped flowing into my life.

It's been said that two good indicators of someone's priorities are a person's checkbook and appointment book. In other words, take a close look at how important money is to you and take a careful look at how you're spending your time.

Now, if you're beginning to understand the cost of commitment, you'll need to understand the consequences of establishing those priorities.

A—Accept the Consequences of Those Decisions

When you look at your calendar, you have to ask yourself tough questions, such as: "How much do I value time with my wife and my kids?" Sacrifice of your own discretionary time will be a major consequence of committing to your family. It costs time and many other things to be committed.

The consequence of sacrificial love is that it will cost us time and money. It will cost us personally and professionally. Commitment requires sacrifice that puts aside self-interests. Do you want to take the road of commitment or convenience? In marriage and in family life, is what I do convenient or does it show commitment? This isn't a trial program. It's not a pair of shoes you take on and off or exchange for another. Commitment is not like a quick stop at the convenience store where you just pick up a few things you need to get by for a while.

Commitment commands a big price up front. I've had the privilege to spend time with a lot of "seasoned folks"—the elderly. I've never heard one of them say, "Gee, I wish I'd spent more time at the office!" Instead they look back on their lives and say "I wish I'd spent more time with my family. I wish I would have made it to more dance recitals, more games, more special events. I wish I would have spent more time in the backyard, more time camping, hiking, fishing, reading, just hanging out with my kids." Don't live your life only to regret what you didn't do with your children. Invest your life now—not tomorrow, not next week, not next year.

Y—Yield the Benefits

Time invested in our families will yield benefits that will never be a disappointment. We'll yield benefits sometimes now, but most often down the road. I'm not presumptuous enough to paint an unrealistically pretty picture of parenting. Kids are like a Certificate of Deposit you invest in. Sometimes after a year or two of investment, you get a small return. Other times parenting is like putting resources into an IRA—you don't see the returns until many years from now. But what you do each day is still an important investment in your kids' lives, resulting in greater communication, greater trust, and greater self-esteem.

Sometimes the values you model don't seem to be showing up in your children. But if you'll pay the price, you'll see results. Someone once said that children aren't very good at listening to their parents, but they've never failed to imitate their parents.

Love in action always protects, trusts, hopes, perseveres. It never fails. And this is the kind of commitment we need in order to make our commitment last.

S—Stick to It

A little boy was talking with his mother one day. In a contemplative fashion he asked, "Mommy, is it true that God created Adam from dust?"

The mom replied, "Yes, Son, that's true."

Then he said, "Mommy, is it true that when we die, we turn into dust?"

Again, she replied, "Yes, Son, that's true."

Then he thought for a minute and said, "Well, Mommy, I just looked under my bed, and somebody is either coming or going."

Maybe you're like me. Sometimes in my parenting, I don't know if I'm coming or going! The responsibility of parenting can be overburdening and overwhelming. If you're ready to quit, I want to encourage you to stick with it. I know that encouragement to hang in there won't flow freely out of your kids! My son has never come up and said, "Dad, I want to tell you how much I appreciate how you keep on me about taking out the trash and cleaning up my room. I understand how this will serve me in the long run."

You can't always count on immediately seeing your commitment lived out in your children. There will be times you'll blow it or drop the ball. And there will be times when your kids come up and kick the ball right out of your glove. But that's when your kids need your love most.

They need your love when they lie to you, when they lose their tempers, when they get caught cheating. They need your love when they don't make the team or the play. They need your love when their hearts are broken, when the sixth-grader they had a crush on ends up liking their best friend. They need your love when they bottom out, when their grades are poor, when they come home stoned, drunk, or pregnant. Commitment to your children demands your love even when they have denied the values you've tried to instill in them.

Perhaps you aren't as committed now as you've been in the past. Don't give up! I'm a guy who has dropped the ball time after time. And I've needed to renew my commitment to my wife and family.

The beauty of building your relationships based on

your relationship with God is that you get a second chance. God says, "I know you're human. I know you lose your temper. I know you really stink at communication. I know you're about as intimate as a bowling ball. But it's all OK. When you renew your commitment, I'll honor it. Renew your commitment and I'll strengthen you."

Perhaps you've blown it. Remember, it's not a knockout blow. God gives us strength and encouragement to go at it again and again and again. In your commitment to relationships, start over fresh if that's what you need to do.

Prioritize your relationship to God, to your spouse if you have one, and to your family. Renew and deepen commitment in your life today. Make sure that it's a commitment, not just a convenience.

Have you heard the story about the pig and the chicken? One day they decided to put on a breakfast for the community. The chicken said, "Let's serve ham and eggs."

The pig said, "That's great. For you, it's all in a day's work. But for me, it's a lifetime commitment."

Raising our families is like that. It takes a lifetime commitment.

1. Earl Gottschalk, Jr., "Orel Hershiser Sees a Lot of Pitches Related to Money," *Wall Street Journal*, 15 March 1989, 51:1a, 10a.

2. Hal Bodley, "Pete Rose's Kids Throw Some Dirt on Dad," *USA Today*, 23 March 1989, 1A.

3. Ibid.

4. Ibid.

Chapter 6

Building a Spiritual Foundation

A few years ago, we moved to Colorado Springs. While I pretty much snored my way through geology class in high school, our move here brought me into conversations about a common soil called "bentonite."

Bentonite is a claylike soil that expands when permeated by water and contracts as it dries out. If you buy or build a house on bentonite, you're in trouble! If it acts up, your doors won't close, your floors can sink six to eight inches, and eventually the whole foundation of your house can be unstable.

You can begin with a gorgeous home that you bought for an unbelievably great price. But if the foundation is faulty, you're going to pay. It doesn't take a degree in geology to understand that what the house looks like doesn't matter if the foundation is sinking.

Why does what seems like a "no-brainer" in house construction not transfer into our parenting skills? When it comes to building the lives of our children, too often we neglect God's instruction to give our children foundations that will last.

Two Different Pictures

If I asked you to sketch what you wish your kids would look like when they're grown, what kind of picture would you draw? Would you color in a blue or pink mohawk? How about tattoos or pierced body parts, or Walkmans permanently affixed to their skulls? Would you dress them in the "grunge" look?

Back in the 1960s, when I was in grade school, my parents probably wouldn't have drawn me with long hair, plaid bell-bottoms, or red high-heeled shoes! But if I were bold enough to print a picture of myself as an eighteen-year-old, that's what I looked like—hair to the shoulders, bell-bottoms, and platforms.

Wouldn't it be great to be able to design and program our kids and send them into the world according to our dreams? We want our kids to look good on the outside. We want them to grow up as clean-cut leaders, involved in the youth group, winners of citizenship awards. Perhaps in your imaginary picture, you would draw your child with a college diploma in one hand and a stethoscope or engineering tool in the other.

Allow yourself to visualize another image. What would you like your kids to look like on the *inside?* Dream about talking to your child and hearing him verbalize some mature discoveries. Perhaps he's learning that his deepest, most intimate love needs cannot be met by a person and he realizes he needs to make a spiritual connection. And he's not looking for another spiritual fad or guru, but rather a personal, intimate relationship with God. Rather than ricocheting from one relationship to another, he's discovering the stability and security of God's love.

Perhaps in this imaginary thought, you see your child's self-esteem is off the charts. He's not deriving his significance from how well he performs. You see an inner peace, not some erratic ball of adolescent emotions bouncing off the walls. He seems to have a greater sense of satisfaction with life. He has a job and he likes it. He enjoys life. Most of all, he actually enjoys God. He makes choices which reflect God affecting his life.

What's the difference between these two pictures? One describes the All-American athlete or scholar who has a secure, well-paying job and looks great on the outside. Maybe he's even sprayed with some spiritual "Armor All." Squirt on a little each week and shine him up to look good for a few days.

The other picture reveals the heart of a child who is becoming filled in his inner being with the love of God. This is an individual who, as Ephesians 3:16-19 describes, is strengthened in his inner being, rooted and established in love. And from an inner self filled with God's love flows noticeable displays of healthy self-esteem, life goals, healthy relationships, and solid values.

So what do you want for your kids? Do you want

them to look good from the outside-in or the inside-out? If internal growth matters most, then the question is: How do you instill the love of God into the lives of your children?

Warning: Don't Try This at Home

Let's look at three popular methods parents have used over the years in well-meaning but misguided attempts to develop spiritual foundations in their children.

Cram and Jam

Force-feeding kids has been a popular choice of some religious parents. These well-intentioned moms and dads have read the books, learned the Bible verses, and watched the seminar videos. They're in "overdrive" as parents. Cram-and-jam parents feed their kids from a spiritual fire hydrant, holding their children over the cap of the hydrant and blasting them with spiritual truth.

Of course, the problem with this approach is that the supply exceeds the demand. Too many of these kids feel gagged by their parents. They have religious teaching and Bible verses crammed down their throats. But when they start asking honest questions regarding the truth and validity of Christianity, their parents can't handle it! The parents become threatened by this kind of interaction.

The reaction of cram-and-jam parents is usually to crank the pressure up on the fire hydrant even more.

Just a few more Bible verses to make the questions go away. Sadly, instead they often end up with disillusioned, bitter kids who enter adulthood wondering how Christianity fits into their lives and if it really makes any sense.

Barbed Wire and Electric Fence

These parents decide that they want to keep their kids out of the reach of the ugly outside world! Just build a wall high enough or a fence secure enough to shelter children from all the harsh elements of life.

I'll admit that this method has been attractive to me. I look at my children and hear stories about what they're exposed to in school. I dream about picking up my family and moving to a deserted island somewhere to protect their innocence. It's tempting to believe that all our family really needs is a roof over our heads, some food—and maybe a satellite dish to get ESPN!

When my teenage daughters were young, I had nightmares about them growing up and dating animalistic boys. So I dreamed about developing an application process to thin out the candidates. After prospective dates filled out the forms, they'd be required to leave a $500 deposit. Of course, I'd interrogate them at the kitchen table while I just happened to be cleaning my gun.

The problem with "barricade" methods is that they're ineffective in the long run. They can provide a temporary sense of security, but eventually our kids grow up and realize there's a whole world out there. And one way or another, they'll break through our fences to explore and experience the world. And we soon discover the instability of their spiritual foundations.

Divine Doormats

Some parents think the most effective way to keep kids on track spiritually is to make them doormats. When kids start to get out of line, "divine doormat" parents step on them and grind them down with healthy doses of guilt and fear. These parents communicate to their kids "that's what God will do to you if you get out of line."

These parents act as God's agents. They say things to their kids like, "You did what? You're not reading your Bible or praying? Boy, I'd hate to be you right now. Don't go out in any lightning storms. You don't know what God might do to you!" Or they'll shame kids with words like, "You said what to your brother? And you call yourself a Christian!"

If you recognize the way you were raised, it might make you laugh now that you're through it all. But a lot of us use these methods with our own kids. And they can result in messed-up, confused, angry kids with big-time spiritual damage.

A Blueprint for Spiritual Architects

If the cram-and-jam, barbed wire and electric fence, and divine-doormat methods can backfire, what are some positive ways to build spiritual foundations into the lives of our kids? Here are three ideas:

Instruction

In Ephesians 6:4, God tells parents: "Do not exasperate your children; instead, bring them up in the training and instruction of the Lord." We've been given responsibility to develop faith and character in the lives of our children. We can't buy into the philosophy that encourages parents just to let kids grow up on their own and develop their own beliefs.

But notice that this verse says "Bring them up." It doesn't say "Drill it in." The idea is wise, progressive nurturing which is age- and rate-appropriate. The supply must not exceed the demand.

Parents sometimes have such an intense desire to see their kids grow in the spiritual dimension that they "do their duty." They get up every Sunday morning and drop off their kids at church! But you can't rely on the church to be the sole provider of spiritual instruction for your children. Add it up for yourself: Your kids may spend up to fifty hours a week watching TV, thirty-five hours a week in school, sixty to seventy hours a week sleeping, and then you put them in church for an hour or two a week? That's barely 1 percent of their time!

Deuteronomy 6:5-7 reminds parents of their responsibility to pass on spiritual truth to their children. We're not to bury them under a constant barrage of spiritual data and information. Rather, this passage reinforces the concept of capturing "teachable" moments. As we "do life," living life with our kids, we pass on truth in natural ways.

Doing life can happen in the simplest of activities.

Never underestimate the impact of a family meal. How can you seize opportunities to share spiritual truth? You can't always plan "teachable moments." They pop up as we're with our families, whether at meal times, on vacations, or just hanging out together.

When I was a kid playing Little League, my dad seized an opportunity to pass on one of the most significant lessons I've ever learned. I was third baseman. A runner was on third, and when the ball was hit and thrown home, the runner knocked over the catcher. The two kids got up and started shoving each other.

Then their dads jumped out of the stands and stood toe-to-toe, swearing at each other in front of all the kids. Then another man jumped out of the stands. It was my dad! He stood between these two grown men and said, "Guys, this is ridiculous! Let's grow up and get back to our seats." I will never forget how proud I felt at that moment. My dad had taught me a lesson in courage. He didn't quote a verse or preach a sermon. But he demonstrated courage to stand up for what is right. He came out of the stands and took a stand.

Are you seizing opportunities to model what's right? Your children need parents who capture moments to come alongside and instruct them. They need moms and dads who make commitments and keep them.

Your children need parents who are committed to God no matter what it takes. Parents who consider the spiritual life of the family so important that you make time to pray and read the Bible with your kids. Parents who have conversations with God, and conversations with other people about God. Parents who trust God with your jobs, your finances, your futures. Parents who go to church and interact with other people who have God at the center of their lives as well.

Interpretation

If you resist the temptation to barricade your kids, then you need to be committed to standing by them as they encounter the world around them. Real-life exposure is unsettling. So you need to help your kids interpret what they encounter.

Maybe these scenes from my life resonate with some of your experiences as a parent. When your little boy is crying in his room because he knows most of the kids in his class will be at a birthday sleepover and he wasn't invited, he needs Mom or Dad to help him negotiate that hurt and feel good about himself.

When your little girl runs for Student Council for her class for three years in a row and doesn't get elected, someone has to be there to tell her she's not a failure, to try one more time or to try something new.

When your daughter has had great friends all the way through junior high and now in high school those friends are making choices she doesn't want to be a part of, Mom or Dad needs to be there to wipe the tears and encourage her as she reconstructs her social life.

Maybe you had a child involved in an extracurricular activity that ended up being a disaster. My daughter started in left field for her high-school softball team. Each year the team went through the same cycle. As the season went on I would watch the coach lose control when the team lost a game. He would bench the upper classmen and bring up younger players and declare, "If I'm going to lose, I'll lose with freshmen." So by the end of each season the seniors were sitting and the underclassmen were kicking the ball around the infield. My daughter has an acute sense of right and wrong and each year it bothered her to see the upperclassmen benched.

When my daughter was a junior, no seniors were naive enough to come out for the team, so when the cycle began again, she was the recipient of the coach's pattern. The pain of being mistreated was nearly a season-long endeavor. I couldn't explain the "why" to my daughter. Like most parents, I wanted to make life right for her. I wanted it to be fair. But life isn't. Like most people, she was learning that the tough way. She was also learning she needed to stick to her commitment to the team, regardless of the coach.

In one practice, the second baseman blew out her knee. So the coach moved my daughter to second—a position she'd never played. She came home from practice and said, "Dad, I know as soon as I make an error, he'll pull me, and he won't put me back in left." I talked to the coach about her concern, but with a warm smile he assured me that wouldn't happen. Sure enough, it happened by the fifth inning of the next game. I wanted to take that coach out behind the school and give him a Bible study he'd never forget!

I walked up behind her on the bench and said, "Honey, if you want to go home right now, I'll walk right beside you."

She quietly said, "No, Dad, I'm going to stay with the team."

I was so proud of her. She could have walked and no one would blame her. But she faced her unfair life experience. That was a tough thing to do, but it was the right thing to do.

Jesus knew this as he nurtured his disciples. He didn't remove them from the world. Instead, he taught them to interpret their culture and to take a stand within it. John 17 records Jesus praying to his Father. He didn't ask that they be taken from the world, but that they be "guarded from the evil one."

Of course, you don't want your kids to get hurt. You'd much rather step in and intervene when life causes them pain. You'd be glad to tell your kid's coach a thing or two when you think he's not treating your child fairly. You wish some parent-teacher conferences were about two hours long so you could tell your child's teacher exactly how to teach your child right.

But what your kids need most are parents who help them interpret the injustices of life. Parents who help them understand that people aren't perfect, and sometimes even people who care about them can be mean. Parents who encourage them to take a stand when they're struggling to line up on God's side, even as they watch their friends line up on the other side. Parents who model integrity in the midst of a generation that's moving farther from God.

As you wisely and carefully expose your children to the real world, you need to assure them that God's love, strength, and presence will be with them as they navigate this journey. Sometimes it will seem easier—and even wiser—to ride in on a white horse and rescue your kids than to go through the "mess" with them. It will seem easier to intercept and take control than to trust God as you wade through the treacherous waters with them.

But over time, you will serve your children best by teaching them to make wise choices. Your greatest joy will come not because they've always obeyed you or behaved perfectly. But as the Book of Proverbs repeats over and over, your greatest joy will result when your children demonstrate that they've learned wisdom.

Consequences

How do we produce wisdom in our children? I wish there were an easier way, but wisdom typically comes as children experience the natural consequences of their choices. When we try to circumvent this process, we rob them of the best institution that can teach them wisdom: the school of experience.

In our home, our teenagers who are driving now, know that if they break the speed limit, they'll pay for their own tickets. And if they lose their licenses, they'll be making arrangements to get around because we're not going to become full-time chauffeurs.

Ann and I know all too well how difficult it can be to allow children to experience consequences. For example, when a teen rejects your family values and systematically chooses to destroy the life of your home, you need to say some hard words: "You may choose to destroy your life, but you will not destroy your brothers and sisters and the life of our home. So if you choose not to straighten up and fly right, then you've made the choice to fly upside down somewhere else."

Delivering this kind of "tough love" message may well be the hardest conversation you'll ever have with your child. And there's still no guarantee it will turn out OK in the end. For us, it did, fortunately. I thank God for that and give him all the credit. But helping your children become wise by letting them experience consequences is not an easy task.

So what do you want for your kids? Will you be content when they have a mild amount of spirituality, a thin veneer of God? Or do you want your children to have God at the core and center of their lives? If so, instruct, interpret, and allow consequences to teach them. God promises that he will be with you throughout the process. Building spiritual foundations in the lives of your children is an investment well worth the effort.

Chapter 7

Home Run: Building Your Child's Self-Esteem

I have been coaching kids in sports since I graduated from college. My favorite sport to coach is T-ball. A lot of sports programs for kids look like this: a lot of kids trying to have fun and a lot of parents trying to ruin it! But T-ball for four- to five-year-olds is different.

T-ball is one of the greatest adaptations of baseball ever invented. In T-ball, a soft covered ball is used. It doesn't hurt if you get hit by it, so kids aren't scared of it. The ball is pitched by the coach to the player, and the player gets three swings at pitches (or I should say the coach gets three chances to hit a swinging bat). If the player doesn't hit the ball, the ball is then placed on a stand—the T—and the player swings until he hits it.

When the ball finally lands in fair territory, the player runs to first. Even if he's thrown out he stays there!

Then the next batter comes up, and the long, often humorous, process starts over. In T-ball, everybody bats one time each inning, no one gets thrown out, and everyone gets to score. Yet no score is kept! Everyone is successful, everyone wins! One of the most exciting rules in T-ball is this: Once everyone has batted, the last batter gets to run all the way around the bases for a home run, even if he hits it back to the pitcher! Everyone longs to be the last batter so he can hit that home run!

I'm very competitive in every sport I play, so I realize T-ball isn't very realistic. But it sure is refreshing. As a T-ball coach, I've never had to yell at one of my players. I've never had a player cry, never a parent complain about his child's playing time, never watched a parent chew out his or her child. Unfortunately, there will be plenty of that later in their life. Every kid gets a chance to step up to the plate, to make it around the bases, and every kid gets the thrill of hitting a home run and crossing home with the team there to "high five" him.

I think parenting should be less like Major League baseball and more like T-ball. What if all children had a chance to "step up to the plate"? Wouldn't it be great if each child could experience the exhilaration of running around the bases of life without getting thrown out? And all kids could have the joy of crossing home with a family team "high fiving" them. Children who experience that kind of opportunity, that sensation of success, and that level of encouragement will have valuable deposits made into the self-esteem reservoirs of their lives.

Some kids are relegated to the bench from the start of life's game. They never get off the bench because they don't feel valued by the significant people in their lives. As we think about our own kids growing up in our homes, we can make sure they have the opportunity to get off the bench, play life's game, and round these four bases.

Stepping Up to the Plate: I'm Valuable

The most important message we can send our kids is that they are the most valuable gift in the world. Most parents feel this way, but struggle in their ability or comfort level to instill that message. Building your children's self-esteem is all wrapped up in affirming their value. Your children need to know that they are valuable to you—not for what they can accomplish, but just for who they are.

That's a tough thing to communicate. It seems more natural to notice when our kids are doing well. It seems natural to high five them for a home run—and there's nothing wrong with that. But if that's all they get, then the message is one of praise and back slaps for proficiency in performance.

That's the message your kids will hear the rest of their lives from peers, employers, and everyone else. When was the last time your boss came up to you and said, "I just want you to know that you are valuable to this company simply for who you are, not just for what you do for us"? You'd probably wonder what he or she was really up to.

Children need to know that no matter what happens when they're up to bat in life, they'll have the same value when they return to the bench to face the family team. With that feeling of security, they won't be afraid to step up to the plate again and again. The strong self-esteem that is built will make kids better performers in life!

Now wait a second! Isn't performance supposed to be left out of the equation? Yes and no. Here's the principle: Your love and value for your children is not contingent upon their performance. But the degree to which you violate it will be the degree to which your children's self-esteem is adversely affected.

If you lavish your love and value on your children without strings attached, they'll develop a strong self-concept that will lead to stronger relational skills and responsibility. Their healthy self-concept prepares them for success in the classroom, at home, and at the playground. Children tend to have greater learning capacity, relational capacity, and responsibility when they feel good about who they are. They need to feel their value, to sense that they really matter regardless of GPA, ERA, SAT, or ACT.

One thing that has helped me focus on this part of parenting is my "Just Because" dates with my kids. One fall afternoon I showed up at my son's classroom and took him out of school. When he saw me he wondered what was wrong. I just smiled and said, "Let's go!" I never told him where. I just had his bag and fishing pole packed and we took off. Two hours later we landed at a lakeside cottage where we fished and had fun for a couple of days—just because. No reason necessary, no motivational purpose—just because.

It doesn't have to be this extensive. A bouquet of flowers delivered to your daughter at school, an ice cream after soccer practice, a new outfit for the recital—anything that doesn't demand an occasion or obligation. Just because! When your kids begin to understand they are loved and valued "just because," it provides a tether between your heart and theirs.

Another responsibility parents have in building strong self-esteem is to make sure their children know someone besides Mom or Dad values them. Unbelievably, someone loves them and values them even more than Mom or Dad. When children begin to get a grasp of how much they are valued by their parents, then they catch a glimpse of how much they are loved by the One who loves them most—the God of the Universe! Kids need to know that they are valuable to their Creator. God didn't create them because he was particularly bored one day and had nothing else to do. They were created out of the love in his heart. God didn't need them, he just wanted them! And he takes great joy in seeing his children grow in their self-esteem and understanding of life.

Value—no matter what my performance. Love—with no strings attached. That's tough to do. But our children need to know that they're just as valuable when they strike out as when they clear the bases. Parents who want to see their kids hit "home runs" in life will constantly, creatively, and continually send the message that they love and value their children.

First Base: I'm Gifted

For some parents, one of the great ego watershed issues they face is this: "Is my child gifted?" As a father of five, I've had to go through those years of testing with my kids. Parents get together and talk about the results of the testing. You can see their chests expand a little when they mention that Bobbie was tested as gifted.

On the other side of the equation is the shallow, sometimes depressing feeling parents have when their child doesn't test as "gifted." "Well, I guess Sarah will just be 'average' then the rest of her life." You may not say that, but that feeling probably crosses your heart and mind at some time.

Well, here's the truth: There are no average kids! Every child is gifted. All children have been given special abilities coupled with a unique design that gives them an edge on being successful in life. None of my children are gifted or skilled in all the same areas. One is a tremendous thinker, another extremely persevering. Another has terrific relational skills, another has a zest for life, another has a gentle and tender spirit. All of my children possess gifts and skills to negotiate life successfully. I just have to recognize where they are gifted! If you want to build your children's self-esteem, you have to send messages to your children that if they use the gifts and talents God gave them, they will be successful. Make your children aware of the fact that they already possess the essential ingredients for success in life.

How do you identify the gifts and abilities your children have? You probably aren't going to like my answer:

Take twice as long to clean the garage next Saturday as you planned. Or how about this one: Make twice the mess in the kitchen next time you cook. It gets worse: Next time you're making a plaster volcano or a model rocket for the science project—spend twice as long making it and create twice the mess. How do you do this? How do you waste valuable time and energy and make any project more difficult? Just ask your children to join you.

So many parents want to approach the task, get it done, and check it off the list. That's the way I'm wired. So when Jordan wants to build a teepee for his Native American unit, I better plan on it taking about twice as long as it would normally take me alone. If you're like me, you fixate on the finished product rather than the process of growing and learning. But when you do that, you rob your kids of the focus necessary for them to grow and develop. If you ask them to "just stay out of the way now" too often, they end up having a negative view of their talents and abilities. They won't really discover where they are gifted. This impedes their self-confidence and puts them behind in life skills.

You might be thinking, "Yeah, but what about quality? If Jason helps me paint the bedroom, I'll have to do it over as soon as he goes to bed." And you might. But even during the task, you can teach and have fun—without passing judgment on his work. "What a great job of painting, Jason! But we aren't painting the carpet right now. Let me show you how to clean that up." You get the picture—that's the way kids identify their gifts, their talents, their propensities. And they love to discover them doing things the way adults do. That's how they learn.

Here's a simple exercise to do with your kids. When you lie down with them at night, you can affirm their value and their giftedness by simply asking them:

"If you had no homework for a week, what would you like to do after school?" (And watching TV is not an acceptable response.)

"If you could do one thing with Mommy or Daddy, what would it be?"

"What do you think you do as good as anyone else?"

Then take the time to share with them:

> "I think you're just about the best ____________ I know!"
>
> "I think God has given you a special ability to ___________________."
>
> "If I were going to _________________, I'd want you there with me."

Second Base: "I Don't Need to Be Perfect"

If you are a perfectionist, you just got an ulcer. If you are an obsessive-compulsive, you've probably already shut the book. If you're already more laid back in life, you just said, "What's the big deal?" For balance, then, could I add a tag on this title?

"I don't need to be perfect—just diligent."

If there's one place I've really struggled in my parenting, it's been in the area of expecting too much from my kids in their performance. I tend to be a perfectionist. I have high expectations of myself. You could fill volumes of psychological journals as to why I'm like this, but no need to discuss that now. I just know that I am, and I tend to transfer my perfectionist expectations onto my children. But I've found that nothing challenges perfectionism like children. I think it's God's sense of humor coming through.

Before I deal with parental perfectionism, I want to comment on the laid-back, nonengaging approach to parenting. While we shouldn't be perfectionistic or demand it of our kids, we also shouldn't leave our children's accomplishments to default. Some parents—either in an attempt to be balanced or because they're lazy—don't encourage their children's efforts whatsoever. If their children get discouraged, frustrated, or just plain tired of working toward a project, laid-back parents may see it as their duty to relieve the pressure and stress from their children. But what those kids really need is a lesson in diligence. These life lessons have become clichés, but they're still true: You don't give up when you get discouraged. You don't jump ship at the first sign of water. You don't give up baseball because you strike out.

The virtue of diligence is something our children must learn. Our kids need to learn to be finishers. Following through on commitments and projects makes deposits into a child's self-concept account and builds valuable character qualities like trustworthiness, discipline, and confidence. These investments, placed into the lives of children, yield tremendous dividends throughout the rest of life.

However, kids are kids. They aren't little Disney

movies about overcoming all odds. Kids are not the extension of our dysfunctional perfectionism.

My wife taught me a lesson early in parenting that goes something like this: "White shirts wash." When my kids were younger, I loved to come home and play with them. The problem with toddlers is that they are always wearing or carrying part of their lunch. Inevitably, I'd get jelly, Kool-Aid, or chocolate somewhere on my white shirt. Eventually, I'd walk in the door and stiff-arm my kids instead of hugging them. When Daddy walked in, they were trained to march to the bathroom and wash their hands instead of running to me like they wanted to.

OK, that's easy. I'll lighten up and do laundry a bit more often. But what about those rooms? Good grief, you could lose a body in my daughter's room. Or what about their grades? They're smart enough to do so much better. And what about their . . . and on it goes.

Now, I'm afraid to say what I'm about to say because it could be used in a court of law—by my kids. Or they'll avoid the judicial system and blow up a copy of these words and tape them to my bathroom mirror, refrigerator, computer, car door, and TV. As a perfectionist dad, I find myself always tweaking the tasks that my kids do. Sometimes with comment, sometimes without. Whether or not I make a corrective comment as I adjust their not-quite-perfect work isn't the point. They still get the message: "I can't do it good enough."

Constant correction or perpetual tweaking can lead to habitual discouragement for our children. I have to work on this one principle: Focus on the learning process, not the end result. I must resist the temptation to pass excessive judgment on their work while they're in the learning stage. If I constantly focus on getting my desired end result rather than developing their field of experience, then I end up damaging their self-confidence. My kids will stop asking me to be a part of their projects. They'll do them while I'm gone to work or behind closed doors. Instead of including me in that important part of their lives, they'll make themselves scarce.

The Bible offers a wise warning for hypercritical or overinvolved parents:

> Fathers, don't exasperate your children by coming down hard on them. Take them by the hand and lead them. (Galatians 6:2, TM)

Where do we lead them? Do we lead them where we want them to go or do we lead them where they need to go next? Moving on to third base helps provide a run around the bases of life that will infuse esteem and confidence into your child that you haven't seen yet. Third base covers the area of making a difference in the world.

Third Base: "I Can Make a Difference"

It was an unusual but refreshing experience. My kids were going through their "stash of cash" hidden in their unique safety deposit boxes. Devon had her pennies, a bit of silver, and a few George Washingtons crammed in her music box on her dresser. After an hour of searching, Jordan remembered where he had put his stash—it was behind his dart board. My two youngest were quite excited to count their money on this Sunday afternoon. At first, I thought they were using that built-in kid radar to detect the approaching ice cream man driving his ugly vehicle with that awful rendition of "The Entertainer" playing ad nauseam.

But no. As I eavesdropped, I heard them talking about the little girl in the Third-World country named Helena they were sending their money to. That morning in Sunday School, the class had adopted Helena to support for the next year. Something about this project had moved their little souls and caused them to realign or reevaluate their values.

When kids (or adults for that matter) realize that they can be a part of something bigger than themselves, it touches them. When kids believe that their dollars, their time, their volunteering, their own uniqueness can make a difference in the world, it means something to them. Too many kids are surrounded by an environment or system that emits the constant message, "get, get, get." "Get what you can. Take care of yourself. Worry about yourself. If everyone did that, there'd be a lot less problems." This kind of thinking is counterproductive as parents try to develop children who have a proper worldview that builds a healthy self-esteem.

Making a difference in the world depends on your children's self-perception. Their self-perception must be molded with enough success stories to establish a confidence to live, compete, win, and fail in their world, and still stay in the game. You need to send the message to your children that they have the skills, abilities, and aptitude to be a success in the classroom, at the Scout meeting, on the playground, or at home.

One volunteer position I picked up was that of Scout leader. I've always enjoyed working with kids through Scouts, baseball, basketball, or soccer. I love to see children succeed. But I'm not sure where Donald is going to end up. Donald has Attention Deficit Disorder, but that's not his biggest obstacle. His biggest obstacle is his dad. We all know that kids love to answer questions that leaders ask. They may know the answer or they may not have a clue! Kids just like to raise their hands. Donald is one of these kids. When I ask our group a question, his hand shoots up. Then his eyes move toward his dad to see if he's going to get the same demeaning line he usually gets: "Why do you have your hand up? You have no clue what the answer is." Time after time Donald is put down. And if I call on him and he doesn't have the right answer, the cuts and insults grow larger.

When children are sent the message they don't have the tools to be successful or live with constant criticism, then they become self-fulfilling prophecies. But when children are given the room to develop, to make mistakes, to become confident in what they do have to offer, they begin to blossom. They become more self-confident, and they become more valuable to society's team—that inherent feeling we all have to be part of something larger than ourselves. To make a difference, children need to know they can be a part of something bigger than themselves.

This whole concept of building your children's self-esteem and self-confidence is extensive. Building your children's self-esteem can be tough work, but it's not impossible. Your children's self-esteem starts out with their understanding of their intrinsic value and worth as someone uniquely created by God and loved and valued by you. The beginning source of information is you the parent. No one can make deposits into the self-esteem banks of your children like you can. The growing emotional health and formation of your children's self-esteem is a priority issue. As they feel confident, they'll be able to "do" life—handle setbacks, deal with rejection, live with successes, and obtain their goals.

Chapter 8

Raising Kids without Raising Cain

Do I call my therapist? Do I call 911? Or should I just solve it all by calling the adoption agency to see what the going rate is for my kids? Do you ever feel like that? For those of you who say you do, you're in pretty good company. For those of you who don't, I can recommend a good "Liars Anonymous" meeting in your region.

Are you tired of the yelling matches with your kids? Are you tired of watching your heart rate skyrocket and your blood pressure boil? I know of few things that bring me greater joy than my children, but the stresses and strains of the business world sometimes seem far more manageable than trying to be a good parent. You love your kids, yet they drive you nuts. You try to stay calm and ask them to "do their chores," and it's like you've asked the cat. You've told them that their homework comes before TV, yet they continue to suffer from periodic short-term memory loss. You bite your tongue, and try again—another command, another demand, another ultimatum, another threat—and you mean it this time!

How can you raise your kids without raising Cain? How can you teach your kids respect, responsibility, obedience, and all those other virtues you want them to grow up knowing if you can't even get them to clean their rooms? Most of us share these frustrations as we negotiate the maze of parenting. If we can't control our children when it comes to things as simple as eating what's served at dinner, how can we control them in more significant areas? That's the challenge—the issue of control.

Control: The Great Wrestling Match of Parenting

It doesn't take a new parent long to realize that those bubbly bundles of beauty you bring home from the delivery room will soon be Wrestlemania Champions in their efforts to control you. Some parents simply give up—and let their children control every aspect of their lives. Other parents are on a mission to show their kids who's the boss. These parents try to control every area of their children's lives. In the first case, you end up with spoiled brats. In the second, you end up with anger-filled tyrants. Parents who try to totally control their children end up losing all control after a decades-long wrestling match.

The secret formula for a healthy survival in this control struggle is found in shared control. Parents have to learn what control to hang onto and what control to give away to their children. If you try to control everything, you'll always be locked in battle with your kids. If you allow your children to control everything, there will always be chaos. Instead, ask yourself, "What is it that I need to control?" and "What areas can I relinquish control to my kids?" These questions assume that you'll make age-appropriate decisions, but the sooner you begin to allow your children certain amounts of freedom and control over their lives, the sooner they begin to understand independence, cooperation, responsibility, consequences, and other elements that lead to maturity.

Of course, you don't start off treating your kids like little adults. We have some friends who have two children—one six and one three. These two kids are probably the most articulate, conversant, and argumentative kids we know. The kids are talked to, catered to, and given permission to act like miniature adults. That's great when everything goes their way. But when I tell the six-year-old he can't climb on the top level of the fort in our backyard, then he has a discourse for me you wouldn't believe. It boils down to this: "Who do you think you are, telling me what to do?"

Children given too much control turn into tyrants. They control their parents in one way or another—through words, guilt trips, tantrums, or tears. And these unhappy kids will grow to be unhappy adults. Relinquishing control calls for wisdom. Two-year-olds can be given the choice of drinking orange juice or milk with their breakfast. But they aren't given the choice of riding their tricycles in the street. Three-year-olds may be given the choice of riding their tricycles in the garage with the door down, or on the sidewalk with Mommy or Daddy beside them. But they shouldn't be given free rein of the remote control. Five-year-olds may be given the choice to have a sleepover or go to Chuckie Cheese for their birthdays. But they can't set their own regular bedtime. Seven-year-olds may have the choice of doing their homework as soon as they walk in the door or getting it done right after supper. But they aren't given the option to save their homework for before school the next morning. Nine-year-olds may have the option of how they want to spend their allowance, but they can't sign up for eighteen record clubs.

Control through Choices, Not Commands

Raising kids without raising Cain means that you understand what wars to wage! You understand levels of control and learn to relinquish it in certain areas. Choices—not commands—provide you with the control you need and allow you to relinquish the control you don't need. When you give your children choices, they're involved in controlling the results and the consequences.

Choices, not commands, work. As the parent, you set limits and eliminate a lot of the wrestling match. More time is spent in dialogue than in fighting. It brings with it the discipline of critical thinking—both on your part and your children's. Coming up with clear, reasonable options takes thinking. You don't say to your children, "You can either eat your dinner now, or you can eat it sometime next week when we next feed you." That's a threat, not an option. What you might say is, "You can either eat dinner with us now, or you don't have to. You can just join us for breakfast tomorrow morning since you aren't hungry." This kind of choice puts the child into the role of decision-maker.

We make sure that we eat dinner as a family nearly every night. When dinner hits the table there are only a few expectations. First, no complaining about the food. Second, you eat what's presented, not your own special meal. If you don't like what's for dinner, I hope you enjoy breakfast tomorrow! I've heard many parents complain about their kids not eating the meals they cook, "They only want peanut butter and jelly" or "They only want macaroni and cheese." It's obvious who's been controlling mealtimes in those homes.

One evening just a few months ago, one of my kids designed a fabulous architectural display—complete with green bean bridges and a gravy reservoir—out of the meal on his plate. When I asked him to stop playing "Bridge Over the River Kwai" with his food and eat, he said, "I don't like this, Daddy."

I responded as any intelligent parent would, "Son, you've eaten this meal before, don't tell me you don't like it."

If this conversation sounds familiar to you, you know that logic means nothing to a child who doesn't want to eat his dinner. He's already thinking of his next line: "I'm just not hungry, Daddy."

This is when it hit me, "Don't debate, don't command—just give choices." So I did. I said he could either eat dinner now or—since he's not hungry—just eat a nice big breakfast in the morning. There was no rebuttal from him for a while. He thought about it as he looked at the cookies for dessert and thought about the bedtime snack he might get if he ate his dinner. But even those "dangling carrots" didn't break his will. He took the option of foregoing dinner—with the hopes that Dad might renege or softhearted Mom might slip him a string cheese or yogurt when Dad wasn't looking. But the night came and went. Morning dawned and I cooked him a nice homemade meal of Lucky Charms. They never tasted so good to him!

Choices work because they eliminate many control struggles. They teach children to do critical thinking and how to live with the consequences of their choices. They also put the responsibility of decisions on the kids, not on the parents. And an important goal of parenting is to see our children grow in their critical thinking—to build a pool of wisdom to draw from. It's like one father, Solomon, said to his son:

> Dear child, if you become wise, I'll be one happy parent. Oh, listen, dear child—become wise; point your life in the right direction. (Proverbs 23:13, 15, TM)

Of course, your children aren't going to agree with all the options or choices you offer them. Kids often won't agree, and they'll crank up the guilt by saying things like, "If you really loved me, then . . . " or "What kind of parent would starve his child?" or "That's not fair" and just about anything they can think of that will push your buttons. Are you ready for that? To be ready, try the following:

1. Don't blow up! Don't engage them, just be clear about the choices.

2. Repeat the choices in a clear but loving way. Don't let them negotiate you down.

3. Stick to your guns—don't back down.

4. Follow through—if you aren't willing to let your child suffer the consequences of the choice, don't offer it.

Let me illustrate this last point through a story that's not quite as humorous as missing a meal. It was probably the hardest decision Ann and I have ever had to make in our lives. I mentioned it earlier, and I write in detail about it in chapter 10, "Parents in Pain." Our son was going through tough times and was choosing to follow his own path—which was rapidly heading in the wrong direction. He was destroying himself, his future, and our family. We went through the entire process of dialoguing, counseling, environmental alteration—and nothing was working.

Long story short and complex made simple. We sat down with our seventeen-year-old son and put the choices on the table. The conversation went something like this: "Son, we love you. We want you in our home, and we want to have a great relationship with you. But you're making choices that are destroying you and eroding our family. Because we have to protect our family, you have a choice to make. You choose to live in our house in the appropriate way, or you find someplace else to live because you will not be allowed to live here anymore."

And for the next several hours he tried to get us to change our minds. He yelled, he cried, he debated, he guilted. But we chose not to engage, we just kept repeating the choices because we had thought the situation through thoroughly. And Ann and I were on the same page. It was a scary choice to offer him, but we were willing to allow him to suffer the consequences and we didn't back down. Was it easy? Of course not. Did he change his mind and straighten up? No, he chose to leave. Was it painful? Yes. The most painful moment of our lives. He was out of our home, living in a detention facility, group home, or on the street during that time. There were months when we didn't know where he was. Did it ultimately work? Yes, it did. And if forced into that situation, I'd do it the same again.

It worked because he had to take responsibility for his own actions. He couldn't blame us for his choice. He experienced the consequences and it ultimately brought him back around.

He has never blamed us for that situation. He's never been bitter toward us or implied that we did the wrong thing. In fact, it has become a tremendous maturing and learning opportunity for him—as mistakes often are!

Mistakes Pave the Path for Opportunity

It's natural for parents to keep their kids from making mistakes. This desire is driven from several different emotions. We may want our kids to be perfect—or close. Unrealistic, but not unprecedented. We may want them to be successful. Nothing wrong with that! We may think that their mistakes reflect our poor parenting. That's a feeling of insecurity, but it's understandable to feel that way. Or, we may want to spare our kids the pain they'll experience. What good parent wouldn't want to spare his child the pain of mistakes? It's only natural.

Unfortunately, many parents believe they're showing love for their kids when they step in the middle of their problems and try to solve them. I think this is the toughest area of parenting. I've found the greatest challenge in my parenting is knowing when to step in and when to butt out. When it comes to intercepting the pain of my children, how far should I go? I spend a lot of time on my knees praying for wisdom in this area. The Bible says:

> Get wisdom—it's worth more than money; choose insight over income every time. (Proverbs 16:16, TM)

> If any of you lacks wisdom, he should ask God who gives generously to all. (James 1:5)

As a parent, I've often made the mistake of trying to stop my children from experiencing pain. But by doing this, I might be impeding the growth they need in life.

When we lunge into the middle of our children's problems, we end up doing our children a tremendous disservice. Our presence can mean a missed opportunity for our child. We steal away the chance for maturing, for learning greater responsibility. And in the meantime, we establish an environment for future irresponsibility.

We need to learn the wisdom of "getting out of the way." We can't solve all of our children's problems. If we intrude into their lives and make their problems our problems, we create an unhealthy situation—for us and for them. Kids who learn to take responsibility for their own problems are motivated to solve them.

My high school daughter had grown to the age where she was too cool to ride the bus. Obviously, my stories of walking to school five miles in the snow, uphill both directions, barefoot, and all that usual baloney didn't matter. We did tell her that we paid taxes for the school system and the bus ride, so don't ask us for a ride. If she didn't want to ride the bus, she'd have to arrange her own transportation. This usually came through a friend.

Now she also had a tendency to beat the snooze button on her alarm clock to death. So there were occasions—increasingly—where she was either late to school or had no ride. It came to the point one morning when she came flying downstairs with that used-to-be-irresistible puppy dog look of, "Dad, loving father, provider of family needs and revered patriarch, could you give me a ride to school?"

To which I replied, "Gladly. I'll be going right by there at about 11:45 this morning. I have a lunch appointment not far from the school!"

To which she replied, "Yeah, but I have classes starting now."

To which I smiled and repeated, "I'd love to drop you off at 11:45."

To which she replied, "Well, would you write a note excusing me?"

To which I replied, "I'd love to write a note for you telling the truant officer that you overslept and didn't arrange a ride and that's why you're late."

I think you see where this is going. Anything we fix for our kids they won't learn to fix for themselves.

Boundaries

If you think that allowing children to have choices and backing off the "drill sergeant mode" means that you don't set boundaries or parameters for effective parenting, then hang on. Establishing boundaries is not contradictory, but is congruent with what we've already discussed about choices.

Setting and enforcing boundaries in the lives of our children is an absolute must if they're to grow into responsible, healthy, and secure contributing adults in society. Some parents have no trouble at all setting boundaries and establishing walls. In fact, some walls resemble the great works like the Berlin Wall and the Great Wall of China. For these parents, setting boundaries for their children is a piece of cake. Other parents have walls made out of cake or Jell-O. These boundaries crumble or melt with the slightest cry, whimper, whine, or tantrum.

We went to a children's movie one time with a single mom who had a handful of problems—her seven-year-old in her right hand and three-year-old in her left. It was an event just waiting in the long line to get in. The three-year-old was not about to do anything he was told. He wandered everywhere, and when his mom tried to contain him, he pitched a fit. Mom came armed though, with about every known piece of bribery equipment known to junk food connoisseurs or toy distributors. If you can't control them, bribe them. When we finally got into the movie I knew there was no way a theater seat would contain him. I thought duct tape would be one solution, but probably not an option. So during the movie he was talking, yelling, and working the aisles more than the ushers. The mom never even saw the movie, and the rest of us only saw part of it. And the three-year-old was all smiles. He had controlled everybody in that theater! What a job.

On the way to the car after the movie, he was a well-behaved little guy. His mom told him to stop and look both ways. He did. He didn't argue, fight, or taunt her the way he had in the theater. When she saw the surprised look on our faces, she said, "Oh, he knows better than to mess around in the parking lot. He knows what he'll get if he acts up here."

Wow! The problem? Mom's struggling with consistency in setting boundaries. And kids see right through that. They'll not only push those limits, but they will ultimately begin to lose respect for inconsistent limit- and boundary-setters. Children who are exposed to consistent, reasonable, and enforced boundaries become secure in their lives. They begin to develop self-confidence and act more responsibly. If we fail to provide boundaries, our kids experience insecurity, and behavioral problems typically ensue.

Communicating boundaries is as important as setting them. We all know that the best noncommunicated idea is as bad as having no idea at all. Parents tend to increase volume with the seriousness of an issue. That means that we are lacing our comments with more anger and frustration. The increased volume-level usually reflects and increases our ire level. It also means that the louder we get, the more firm the limits become. That's what creates the problem. Then our kids start to listen to us only when we get amped up. They don't take us seriously until we get a little steamed.

Raising kids without raising Cain means that when we set boundaries, we speak in a consistent volume. We avoid threats. We offer options. Threats are a funny thing. We use them to intimidate our kids, to make them believe that we are really serious. And sometimes threats work, but sometimes they don't. You may threaten your child: "Either you clean your room or you'll lose your allowance." Some kids will be up in a second shoveling out their room. Others will go, "Big deal." Threats are different than consequences of choices. Threats are directly our mandate; consequences are the choice of the child. Threats usually carry a pejorative tone. That's counterproductive. With consequences, we can calmly follow up on the violations of the boundaries and choices with the same calmness we presented them.

One serious area of boundary-setting in our house deals with the respect with which we speak to one another. Our kids—no matter what age—are not allowed to address us or each other with a belligerent or disrespectful tone. But, as you know, it happens. I used to respond by getting mad and speaking back disrespectfully to them because of the disrespect they were showing. I finally realized that's not too smart! It doesn't work and it's inappropriate. If I don't model respect, how can I expect it in return? Proverbs makes it clear what harsh language does to people:

> Rash language cuts and maims, but there is healing in the words of the wise. (Proverbs 12:18, TM)

I've learned to interrupt my children calmly and remind them that we want to hear what they are saying, but we won't listen to them as long as they're using an inappropriate tone or volume level.

It also works when our kids are speaking to each other. I'll walk into the middle of a sibling argument. The temperature's high and the verbiage sharp. I used to yell at both offending parties and send them to their rooms.

"And you sit there and think about the mean things you said to your brother." The plan is supposed to be that after sitting locked in their rooms they start to soften, their hearts start to melt, and the tears of repentance begin to flow. And they'll run out of their rooms, toward each other, and embrace in sibling reconciliation. Right? No, the longer they think about what they've said, the more time they have to come up with better insults.

I've learned to put the two warring factions in the same room to talk through their issues. If they sit there until morning, fine. But they can only come downstairs once they've become civil with one another and feel they each have been heard. I'm always willing to referee, but only if they can't work it out. What is demanded in this settlement is respect, not resolution.

Parents must insist on respect and obedience from their children, but it comes through a different process than intimidation. It comes through establishing of boundaries. It occurs by giving choices through loving, yet firm communication that avoids the acidic adjectives and tone. It comes through allowing the consequences to be the teacher, to be "the heavy." Let your children's choices and the consequences provide the disciplining necessary.

Consequences with a Heart

This may seem like a silly story to some, but others will understand where I'm coming from. There's a standing joke about disciplining children: "This is going to hurt me more than it hurts you." But I've really felt that. On one Friday night we were struggling to get one of our kids into bed. After all, it was Friday night, no school the next day. But there was a basketball game. I was his coach and he was one of our stronger players. I laid out the choice and the consequence: He really could choose not to go to sleep. But if he did, the consequence was that he wouldn't play in the game.

He chose to keep playing around at bedtime. I'm sure he was thinking, "Would Dad really not let me play? After all, if anyone knows how important basketball is, it's Dad!" Well, I didn't play him. And it hurt—not because we lost. I actually don't remember if we won or lost. It hurt because he loves to play basketball and I love to watch him play. It hurt because he had made a choice I knew he'd regret, but I had to let him make.

Consequences are tough. But they're also great teachers. Choices and consequences leave kids thinking seriously about their behavior and their responsibilities.

Sometimes, as in this case with my son's basketball game, a parent has to impose consequences. Sometimes we impose consequences out of anger so they're not really appropriate. "I told you if you came home late again, I'd ground you. You're grounded until the Cubs win the pennant." Of course, we all know when that will be!

Consequences have to "fit the crime." And they need to be established in love, not shrouded in anger or packaged in threats. Consequences have to be communicated to children so there is a clear connection between the behavior and the consequence.

But consequences are most effective when they flow naturally. Just last weekend I took my two youngest children to the park to fly model rockets with the Cub Scout troop I lead. Here in Colorado, a sunny and warm day means nothing. The weather can change in five minutes when the next front comes over the mountains. I told one of my kids twice, "Put an extra coat in the car." It didn't happen, but the cold breeze started as soon as we got there. She wasn't about to miss out on launching the rockets, but she was cold.

She looked at me and said, "Daddy, I'm cold."

I said, "I bet you are, honey. I'd be cold too if I didn't have my jacket on. Here's the keys, you can go back and sit in the car if you want." I didn't yell at her or tell her, "I told you so." I didn't demean her. She was cold and she knew it!

The real world operates on consequences. When consequences naturally come, they bring with them the cause and effect necessary to make an impression on our children.

Try raising your kids without raising Cain. If your parenting world is full of yelling, screaming, threatening, and "I told you so's," just try this option for a while. When we communicate with our kids in this way, they get the prevailing message that says, "I love you. I value you no matter what you've done. You may have to live with the consequences, but I'm still there for you. I'm still there to go to bat for you."

Chapter 9

Strength for Single Parents

I once heard the story of a woman who'd been married four times. First she married a banker, then a movie star, then a beautician, and finally an undertaker. When asked why, she responded, "One for the money, two for the show, three to get ready, and four to go."

The issue today is not two, three, or four spouses. The issue much more often is zero spouses. One of the greatest challenges facing the family today is that of single parenting.

Awhile back we were spending an evening with a group of friends. It seemed like everyone was having one of those "weeks from hell." A time when everything that could go wrong did go wrong. In the midst of our complaining, one friend said, "I don't know how single parents do it!" That thought resonated with all of us. We were all having a rough time, but we all sensed how much more difficult it must be for a single parent to wallow through everything we were going through.

At first, I thought it was unusual for married couples to have this kind of sensitivity toward single parents. Then I looked around the room and realized that most had been a single parent at one time in their lives, or they had married a single parent.

Almost in a unity of spirit, my friends were baffled at how single parents can survive with the demands placed on them. Like it or not, the world is a different place than it was a generation ago. The responsibility of parenting is much more complex today. The number of plates parents have to spin is difficult enough with two parents in the home, let alone one.

Single-Parent Struggles

God's ideal design for the family is for two parents to lead each family. But the percent of children living in single-parent homes has more than tripled in the last three decades. Today, 17 million children live in single-parent homes. Approximately 90 percent of single-parent homes are homes without a father.[1]

I take so many things for granted as part of a two-parent family. What happens if one of my kids gets sick? I can stay home or Ann can. If I've had a rough day, she can get up and take his temperature; or if she's had a rough day and the kid throws up . . . who cleans it up? I do!

What happens when a car breaks down for a single

parent? Who do they call? And if one of their kids forgets his lunch? Who mows the yard, fixes dinner, does the laundry, goes to the Little League games, reads *Go Dog Go* for the 800th time?

With baths to give, homework to finish, finances to attend to, curfews to enforce, when do single parents find time for themselves? Where's the time for friends? If you're a single parent, you've probably been amazed that some of your married friends have mysteriously misplaced your phone number. You find yourself emotionally drained when your children need you the most emotionally. You find yourself a single parent wondering how to keep your family feeling like family. And you find yourself—when you have time to think about it—wondering what went wrong and who's going to sweep up all the broken plates you've dropped, all the jagged porcelain pieces of your life.

These are just some of the struggles single parents face. They're probably not new to you if you are a single parent—unless you're recently divorced or widowed. As a single parent, you can be successful. It's really quite simple—as long as you are more powerful than a divorce locomotive, faster than the creditors' speeding bullet, able to leap tall laundry piles in a single bound, can bend the steel will of teenagers with your bare hands. That's often what single parents think they have to be—Super Parent.

Greg Cynaumon, in his book *Empowering Single Parents*, talks about the different types or styles of single parents.[2]

Super Parent

Look—up in the sky, it's a bird, it's a plane . . . no, it's a single mom stuck to the ceiling because she's going crazy trying to be super parent. Super single parents try to do everything both a mom and a dad would do. They try to make everything normal for their children. "I'll make sure they're in ballet or boxing—whichever they want. They'll be in all the enrichment programs after school, soccer leagues, YMCA programs, clarinet lessons, and youth group. I'll do it all," she says as she collapses and her kids call 911.

I've got good news and bad news for you if you're a single parent. The bad news—you can't do it all. The good news—even homes with two parents can't do it all! You can't! You're not supposed to do it all.

With the weight of the world on your shoulders as a single parent, don't try to be everything to your kids. You probably feel responsible for and guilty about everything. You feel responsible for your marriage falling apart, for what's going to happen to your kids. You feel guilty about depriving your children of a "normal" childhood. Your guilt leads you to try to be two parents wrapped into one. Super parents typically end up trying too hard. Often, they go to extremes in areas they can control or influence, so ultimately they end up alienating their kids. They mean well, but the problem is simple and out of their control: They can't be both parents at once.

Toxic Parent

Cynaumon says that toxic single parents, like super parents, try to compensate for the missing spouse through their efforts to control. But the toxic parents' means of control is more devastating. The toxic parent employs anger, resentment, and intimidation to manipulate and control the children.

These parents are called toxic because of all the waste and garbage left over from the soured relationship they were involved in. Their bitterness, anger, and resentment falls out on the next closest victims—usually their children. The single parent lashes out when the child shows affection or speaks positively of the ex-spouse or reminds the single parent of the ex-spouse. And in return, the child is the recipient of misdirected rage or is used as leverage against the former spouse.

This style damages children because they never learn the resolution part of conflict resolution. They learn to hang on to bitterness and anger and how to effectively transfer those feelings to someone else. There's never a sense of closure, so moving forward becomes an arduous, nearly impossible task.

Enabler

Remember "Mrs. C.", Richie Cunningham's mother on "Happy Days"? I always wanted to smack her into reality! She was always running around trying to do everything to make Richie and his little sister comfortable. She'd primp him and practically dress him. She protected and babied her children. As long as everyone was happy and "happy days were here again," then everything would be fine. Mrs. C. wasn't a single mother, but I'm surprised Mr. C. didn't turn her into one.

Mrs. C. was the epitome of the enabler, the parent who wants everyone to be happy, everything to work out fine. The enabler thinks, "If I do everything just right, it will all turn out." This type of parent wants the world to be a nicer place. Enablers tend to be overly permissive and fail to set the kinds of boundaries that are necessary for children. The enabler becomes a pushover for children.

Enablers are afraid of being rejected if they're too strict. They've already felt significant rejection from their ex-spouses, so there's no way they want to experience that pain any more. Rejection by their children would be devastating.

A Well-Balanced Single Parent

Which style should you use? First of all, don't throw away the parenting style you had before you were divorced or widowed. Don't change who you are. Of course, you can always improve and develop as a parent. But start by taking the style of parenting you used previously, the style God gave you, the style you have already worked on and developed. Some single parents think they have to trash the ways they used to parent once they're alone with their kids. Don't make the mistake of overcompensating just because you are single now. Utilize your strengths while guarding to make sure you don't push them to extremes. You may have weaknesses as well that you may need to work on—but within your own style.

There's no need for a metamorphosis. Going against the strengths and style God has given you will only create additional difficulties with your parenting. While you don't need to undergo major reconstruction, you might need to make some minor renovations because of your changed circumstances. Remember—you can't do it all. But your circumstances now will require you to do a couple of things. You'll need to "crank up the energy" or reallocate it to focus on some key areas, and you'll need to keep your "antennae up" in order to monitor which of the following areas may need more attention at any point in time.

By the way, these areas are good for all parents, not just single parents.

Display Unconditional Love, Not Idealized Love

Of course, everyone knows you're supposed to have unconditional love for your children. Saying this is about as profound as saying, "You really ought to eat a healthy breakfast." But as a single parent, you need to understand what's going through the mind of a child who has just experienced a divorce. In a way, innocence has been lost, at least the idea that love transcends everything.

Kids inherently believe that love can conquer anything, that love can solve any problem. But children of divorce begin to see love as something that is very fragile. They learn that love is vulnerable to outside attacks. Love becomes so fragile now that careers, money, infidelity, alcohol, drugs, and any other problem can affect it.

None of us wants to withhold our love from our children. But for single parents who have just realized that they will be raising their children without a parenting partner, the timing couldn't be worse. When your kids need the verbalization of your love the most is when you'll least feel like giving it. Understandably, immediately after a divorce or a death, single parents are drained emotionally and may have just experienced the greatest rejection or pain of their lives. But unfortunately, it comes at a time when your children need your love and affirmation the most.

Because of what's marinating in the hearts and minds of children in single-parent situations, single parents must continue to communicate unconditional love and acceptance. A single parent has to view the family from the perspective of the child, especially in a divorce setting where the child has just had his concept of love drastically rearranged.

Because your children's security is being challenged, you need to make every effort to keep the established routine as much as possible. This will be solidifying for them. If there are lessons to go to—they must be attended. If a holiday is to be celebrated—celebrate it. Many single parents find celebrating the holidays the toughest time of their singleness. Often, an overwhelming sense of aloneness creeps in. They think that if they don't observe the holiday or special event, they can protect themselves from those feelings. Single parents especially avoid holidays like Valentine's Day! But even difficult days like this can be a great opportunity to reaffirm the stability of your love for your child without hitting the raw romantic nerve-ending exposed in your heart at this time.

For your children, keeping routines and regularly scheduled events provides connections with a stability that has been disrupted. This connection is so important. No, it won't be the same. Don't try to make it the same or pretend nothing's changed. But the connections will help your children grow through the emotional transition time. Don't forget to keep the "antennae up" to the struggles and failures your child may be experiencing. During this tough transition time, make a concerted effort to verbalize and demonstrate love in the middle of their mistakes.

Use the situation to let your kids know they don't have to be perfect to be loved. This allows them to emerge whole and intact.

Demonstrate Forgiveness

Single parents in the aftermath of divorce need to crank up their willingness to forgive. You need to exercise forgiveness for the person you feel is the cause for bitterness in your life. You're probably saying, "You've gotta be kidding. Forgive the King of Jerkdom? The Empress of Idiocy? The Sultan of Slime? The Princess of Pestilence?"

The Bible is pretty clear about forgiveness:

> Get rid of all bitterness, rage and anger, brawling and slander, along with every form of malice. Be kind and compassionate to one another, forgiving each other, just as in Christ God forgave you. (Ephesians 4:31-32)

There are some negative ramifications of holding on to any bitterness you possess. It not only poisons you, but those closest to you. If you don't forgive your ex-spouse, it will poison your life and affect your children.

Bitterness is something we all experience, but there's basically nothing healthy or good about it. It doesn't really accomplish anything—it just plain doesn't work! A man named Job had every right to be bitter because he had lost all his family, possessions, and wealth. But he understood something about bitterness and resentment.

> To worry yourself to death with resentment would be a foolish, senseless thing to do. (Job 5:2, GNB)

Bitterness can never right a wrong. It only makes the situation worse. Being bitter or harboring resentment can never change the past but it most certainly can ruin your future. Harboring bitterness is like driving down the road with your eyes stuck in the rearview mirror. You're always looking in the past; as a result, you crash in the present.

When you are hurting, you don't need to hurt more. Yet bitterness will hurt you more than anyone you might be angry with. You're boiling over and the person you're mad at may not even have a clue. They're just out, having a good time, enjoying life.

Bitterness isn't worth the cost—the price is too high. You live with "hell in your heart" and it eats you up emotionally. Add to that the toll on your physical health and the price continues to escalate. Bitterness will drain you, cause stress-induced neck pain, back pain, stomach problems, ulcers, and headaches.

The Bible says that resentment will end up killing you:

> Some men stay healthy till the day they die. They die happy and at ease . . . others have no happiness at all; they live and die with bitter hearts. (Job 21:23-25, GNB)

If you're not willing to forgive, you're allowing your ex-spouse to control you, your happiness, and your freedom. Make the choice to forgive. Forgiveness doesn't mean to deny what that person has done to you. Your children need to see that you can forgive your ex-spouse. Then they'll never wonder if there is something they might do that you won't forgive them for.

I think a greater problem than forgiving others just might be our inability to forgive ourselves. You need to forgive yourself. That's not easy to do, is it? Sometimes the person hardest on us is the one in the mirror.

Someone close to me—a person I truly love and admire—went through a divorce. It was the first divorce that ever hit his family directly and they weren't sure how to handle it. The family went from denial to blame to just not bringing it up—ignore it and it will go away. When this friend called to tell me about it, I didn't try to tell him what he did wrong or try to solve his problem. I knew that his greatest problem was going to be forgiving himself. And for years, I watched him walk around in life believing he was damaged goods, convinced he wasn't "worthy" to receive forgiveness from anyone—God, his kids, his family—for his part in the divorce.

A lot of people feel just like my friend. If you've been through a divorce, however long ago it was, you might still feel like damaged goods. But no matter what you did in your marriage, no matter what part you played in the breakup, your Father in heaven forgives you. And when you learn to forgive yourself, then you can be free to be the single parent you were meant to be. If you're unable to receive God's forgiveness and your own, you'll be a hobbled single parent.

Practice Consistency in Boundaries and Appreciation

All children need boundaries. But those in single-parent homes particularly need consistency and predictability. In a home rocked by divorce, children have seen Mom and Dad live through inconsistent relationships, inconsistent communication, inconsistent conflict resolution, inconsistent spiritual support, and inconsistent discipline.

Children who aren't provided with consistency in boundaries will experience greater confusion. Without rules day to day, with constant guessing at what is expected, children don't have much choice except to be confused. They'll want to meet your expectations, but they can't if they don't know what's expected or if you keep changing the rules.

Kids also need to know they're appreciated. If you consistently communicate with them and express your appreciation for their vital role in the family, then you create ownership of the family. With ownership comes a sense of being a valuable part of the team. When children feel part of the team, they'll usually be ready to be part of the solution rather than part of the problem. (Go back to chapter 8 to read more about how to set boundaries—the same principles work whether you're a single-parent or part of a two-parent family.)

Understand Your Child's Hurt

As a single parent, you can't neglect the real pain your children are experiencing after their other parent has left. We tend to minimize the devastating pain this causes kids. Or we rationalize and avoid admitting that children really grieve during this time.

Kids don't know what to do with their feelings. They aren't sure what to do with their hurts or anger. And kids will respond in different ways. Our three oldest children all responded differently when their first dad died. Some kids will withdraw, some will bury their heads in the sand, some will act out, some will get extremely anxious.

If you're single because of a divorce, it may be that

your children aren't ready to talk about your ex-spouse leaving the house and living somewhere else. It may be that they don't want to talk. It's tough to decide when you should try to probe their hearts with questions to find out what's going on. You know your children. If they're not ready, be patient. If they don't want to talk yet—be prepared. Take necessary action steps—including professional counseling—to help them open up.

Here are some ideas and questions that might assist you in working with your children to understand their hurts a little better.

Remind them it's OK to be angry. Even Mom and Dad get angry. It's OK to be angry with Mom or Dad. Ask: "Tell me about what you're feeling. Tell me what makes you angry." Then give them space to be angry without attacking. Teach them how to attack the problem, not the person. You can give them clues to help express how they're feeling: "Tell me how you feel. Sad? Angry? Frustrated?"

Show them that it's OK to feel what they're feeling. Share your similar feelings. Periodically ask the same "feeling" questions. Continually reinforce that the situation is not their fault.

Finally, own up to your end of the problem. Don't pass blame to their other parent. Teach your kids that all people make mistakes, and that it's not a "death sentence" to make mistakes.

Support for You and Your Family

As a single parent, you probably have felt that if you need to seek outside help in times of crisis, you'll be seen as weak or a failure. You already feel horrible without having other people think something is wrong with you if you or your children need to see a counselor.

But the more energy you expend on your family closer to the point of crisis, the greater return you will have on that investment. Unfortunately, there are some good reasons not to expose yourself or the raw emotions that surface during crisis time. It's likely that you have already felt labeled, mistreated, avoided, and made to feel like damaged goods by some in your network of relationships. But as a single parent, you need to rise above that for yourself and for your kids. Isolating yourself from proper counsel and true Christian support will only exacerbate the problems and prolong the recovery time. You need to get yourself and your children into counseling if it's necessary, and you need to plug into a network that will provide the social, emotional, and spiritual support you need.

Above all else during this time, you need to cultivate your relationship with God. Avoid seeking someone else or something else to fulfill you. It will only leave another void in your life. You need to transfer your dependence from people to God.

King David of Israel wrote a popular phrase of poetry that would serve all of us well in our spiritual journey: "Be still, and know that I am God" (Psalm 46:10).

God has a passionate desire to be the center of your life, involved in your parenting, provider of strength during your tremendous challenges and struggles. As a single parent, you'll feel inadequate and guilty. You'll be misunderstood. You are going to be criticized. You're going to be shunned. But look at how King David describes God's care for you:

> But you, O God, do see trouble and grief; you consider it to take it in hand. The victim commits himself to you; you are the helper of the fatherless. . . . You hear, O Lord, the desire of the afflicted; you encourage them, and listen to their cry, defending the fatherless and the oppressed. (Psalm 10:14, 17-18)

Do you feel inadequate? You have a heavenly Father who can make you complete and remove your guilt. He forgives you for whatever mistakes you've made—and even the ones you haven't made yet. Are you misunderstood? He understands you—your hurts, your pain. Have you felt shunned? I'm not sure I've ever met a single parent who hasn't been shunned by someone—a friend, family member, or church member. God never, ever turns his back on you, shuns you, or makes you feel like damaged goods. In his eyes, you are a precious, priceless gem that is beyond human assessment.

Don't give up! "I am on your side," God says. "I'm on your team."

A Compassionate Co-Struggler

If you're not a single parent, you need to read this. I'm hoping you've read this far, even though when the chapter began you might have said, "This is nice, but it doesn't have anything to do with me." If you have read this far, perhaps your awareness has expanded and you're thinking, "Wow, that's too bad." Now I'll suggest that you need to do something more with the information.

My philosophy professor in college felt that Christianity was a sham. He said that to him it was a show, something inauthentic. His reasoning came from a verse in the Bible—a book he otherwise didn't follow or believe in. Over the years, I began to understand why he felt the way he did. The verse is from the letter written by the half brother of Jesus, James:

> Religion that God our Father accepts as pure and faultless is this: to look after orphans and widows. (James 1:27)

There are many noble things to do in life. But here is something that can't be overlooked. God ordained to the rest of us a responsibility to people in this world who need us in their lives to help make them successful in their families.

Don't say, "Well, that's a great idea—it's exactly what the church ought to do!" Don't pass this responsibility off on the church or society. Each one of us has the ability to make a difference. It starts with:

1. Changing our attitude about single parents.

Single parents aren't oddballs; they are co-strugglers. A quick look at our own past reminds us that we aren't blameless individuals either. All of us have our closets, our past mistakes that we may have been fortunate enough to not carry into our present. And we all have struggles and problems in life. We need support ourselves, so it seems natural that a single parent would be in the same position—and the circumstances might even be a little more complicated!

Our attitude change about single parents has to come from within and without. Inside, we need to ask some tough questions: "How can I be more sensitive? How far away am I, really, from where they are? But for the grace of God. . . ." Just like we need to look at all people, we need to see single parents through the eyes of Jesus. It starts within—in our hearts.

We may need to jumpstart our understanding from outside ourselves. Spending time with single parents can make you more sensitive to their situation.

2. Reaching out to single parents.

Supporting single parents means you're involved in their lives. I think that's why Jesus walked among people instead of hanging out at the temple all the time. He was always sensitive and in touch with those who really needed him. When we open our homes and lives to single parents, we begin to understand them in a way that allows us to serve them more effectively.

There are so many practical things we can do for single parents. We can offer to watch their kids just so they can have a night out. We can bring by a meal or two so they can spend less time in the kitchen and more time just enjoying a meal as a family. A single parent might need assistance mowing the grass, fixing the car, doing work around the home. Just a simple invitation to your home for dinner shows single parents—and their kids—that you care about them in a practical way.

3. Becoming a role model for the children of single parents.

When I talk to single parents, particularly single moms, about their needs, they talk about role models for their children. They aren't looking for surrogate parents, just people to spend time with their children. Maybe someone to coach their Little League team or to teach them an instrument. You could take a single parent's kids on a trip to the zoo or a nature center or a ball game. Attend a production at the symphony. Just take the opportunity to get involved in their lives. You possess qualities and characteristics that could be invested into the life of others' children. By doing so, you not only build into the life of the child, you provide a wonderful service to a single parent who is truly in need of the assistance you can provide.

James called this kind of service "pure and faultless" religion. Why? Because there's no return on the investment. Most single parents aren't going to be able to reward you. Their kids aren't always going to be grateful—or even realize what you're doing for them. The service is pure because your motives have to be true. There's no earthly compensation.

So often our society attaches strings to serving other people: "What will I get out of it? What's in it for me? Will this enhance my public image?" It's time for us to stand in the gap for single parents. Their circumstances aren't going away because we ignore them or because we cast blame on people in these tough situations. It's time to serve with no strings attached.

1. "The Index of Leading Cultural Indicators." (1993) William J. Bennett, Washington, D.C.; *Empower America, The Heritage of Foundation*, Free Congress Foundation. Vol. 1, March 1993, 15.

2. Greg Cynaumon, Ph.D., *Empowering Single Parents* (Chicago: Moody Press, 1994), 45–48.

Chapter 10

Parents in Pain

A few years ago, Ann and I struck up a friendship with another couple in our neighborhood. We enjoyed this couple and grew to be close to them—close enough that we began to talk about different issues in our lives.

As we opened up to each other, they shared the struggles they had with their teenager. They spoke openly about the pain, hurt, and distrust that accompanies a rebellious teen.

Ann and I would lie in bed and think about our friends and their pain. We couldn't fathom what they were going through. We couldn't imagine having a child who suddenly becomes a Mr. Hyde. And while we didn't feel superior to them as parents, I think we did presume that something like what they were going through would never happen to our family. After all, we love our kids, sacrifice for them, have instilled strong values into their lives, we've taught them to love God, to love people.

Over the course of one year, things changed. It seemed that one moment our son, Ryan, was sitting around the dinner table teasing his sisters, complaining about doing dishes, wrestling with his four-year-old brother. He was excelling in high school, playing basketball with Dad, planting flowers with Mom. Even at sixteen, every night before bed he would say, "Good night, Mom. Good night, Dad. I love you."

But how things changed in one year. What our family went through was unmatched in our lives. The pain we experienced is indescribable. Ann has said that even the pain of losing her first husband didn't come close to the pain she experienced with our son.

The situation got so bad that we had to appear with our attorney before a judge so the courts could issue a warrant for Ryan's arrest as a fugitive and a runaway. We spent a year praying, counseling with and without Ryan, making trips to group homes, detention centers, and police stations. Yet Ryan made the choice of forsaking our family, our values, and his future.

This chapter is specifically for you if you are in similar pain—or if you very realistically realize that you might feel a similar pain someday. I hope to offer you some encouragement. I can't offer you three steps to getting your child back, or four easy ways to bypass adolescence in your children.

Just some encouragement.

Don't Beat Yourself Up

Parents who've experienced the pain of a child walking out on them, or a child living a defiant, in-your-face life, will at some point begin to beat themselves up. "What did we do wrong? Where did we screw up? Were we too hard on her? Were we too easy on him? Is there something we've done wrong? There must be or else these bad things wouldn't be happening to our son, our daughter."

Do you know what it means to beat yourself up? People do it all the time—not just when dealing with rebellious children, but in other relationships. When we do, we disqualify ourselves from being decent, respectable, honor-worthy parents. We invalidate ourselves.

Invalidation happens because we think we have to find an answer for why our children are rebellious. We think someone should be punished for their rebellion, so it ought to be Mom or Dad. After all, if we'd just been better parents, this wouldn't happen.

Most everyone is familiar with the story of Adam and Eve in the second and third chapters of Genesis. After our struggles with Ryan, this account of original sin took on a whole new meaning for Ann and me.

If you're a hurting parent, read this section of Scripture again. You'll see that God understands just how you feel. When Adam and Eve sinned, God lost his children. God had created them perfectly—no defects, no hereditary problems. He raised them in the right way. He took walks with them. He took them to the zoo—He even created a zoo for them! He loved them unconditionally and perfectly.

He taught them right from wrong, how to make good choices. He clearly warned them of the consequences of wrong choices. But in spite of all that, a negative influence pulled them away from their relationship with their Parent and into rebellion.

When God confronted them, what did they do? They acted like rebellious kids often do today: They were evasive, pointed fingers, and looked for a scapegoat.

Can you imagine the trauma God went through? The pain of losing a relationship with his children whom he loved so much, valued so highly, spent so much thought and care upon? The relationship between God and his children was violated. God was an abused parent, just like many parents are today.

Ann and I felt abused. We felt hurt because the child we loved was headed for self-destruction. We felt abused because we had contributed our lives to this son and he apparently could care less. We hurt because everything we tried to do was spurned initially in subtle ways, yet ultimately in great defiance.

Over time, Ann and I grew to understand that Ryan is no different than Adam and Eve. Ryan was created with the freedom to choose. He knows the choices and he makes the decisions that affect his life—not Ann, not me, not even God.

The beauty of God's creation is that he created us with the freedom to choose. Yet our greatest pain comes from the wrong appropriation of that freedom. When someone else chooses to abuse that freedom, chooses to make wrong choices, we can't beat ourselves up.

God is at the same place we are. He has been there and he hurts with us. If God, who is perfect, raised children who hurt him and rebelled against him, we can't put unrealistic pressure on ourselves. Don't invalidate yourself. Stop beating yourself up.

Keep Up the Farm

Remember the story of the Prodigal Son in Luke 15? I can't tell you how many times I read this passage during our struggles with Ryan. When the wheels started coming off our relationship with Ryan, I read the story again and again. Ann and I would read it over and over, trying to figure out what we could do to "save" our son. We kept reading, thinking we could learn something from this passage to keep Ryan from becoming like the prodigal.

You know what we found? This passage doesn't say a thing about what you can do to stop your children from rebelling. It doesn't say to do anything. What the passage doesn't say finally began to speak to me.

The father never ran after his son. He didn't threaten him, indulge him, or physically restrain him. In fact, when the son finally returned, the farm was still in great shape! It hadn't fallen apart. It was a fully functioning and highly efficient farm just like it had been before the son left.

We have a responsibility to keep up the farm—to keep our home, our health, our relationships, and our employment intact—amidst the storm. Work hard at making sure your home remains a home. Do whatever it takes to make sure your home isn't overrun with weeds, that relationships aren't left to rot, that the responsibilities aren't disconnected, and that your family doesn't go into foreclosure. You must keep up the farm in the midst of your pain.

When the son comes to his father and demands his IRAs, stocks and bonds, and his cut of the living trust, his dad isn't intimidated. The father doesn't roll over and say, "Oh, OK, son, whatever you want. Take it all! Just don't leave." Instead, the father refused to be manipulated by his son with the attitude.

Part of "keeping up the farm" means you learn to deflect intimidation. If you're going to survive as the parent of a rebellious child, you need to deflect intimidation. You must refuse to be manipulated or conned by your child. Your children may threaten you overtly with running away, throwing tantrums, sneaking out without permission, or calling child-protection services. Or they more subtly manipulate you by reminding you that "we live in the '90s," or that "so and so's parents aren't old-fashioned like you," or saying things like "when I turn eighteen, I'm getting out of this prison."

Let me put this simply: As parents, you have your values, your convictions. And provided you aren't a child-beating, drug-abusive, verbally assaultive tyrant, you have the right to expect behavior that is respectful, honoring to God and man, and consistent with the values and priorities your family has established. Don't be intimidated.

Just a note of encouragement. If your children are

sneaking around trying to hide what they're doing wrong, it means they know what is right. If they scheme and lie to avoid getting caught, they clearly know right from wrong. And it means your instruction and influence for positive and constructive behavior is in place and working within them. They're simply making wrong choices that they know are wrong. That's why even in the face of intimidation, you must demand appropriate and constructive behavior.

Maintain Integrity with Your Spouse

Can I offer this encouragement to you if you are married and together you're struggling with a rebellious child? If you're going to make it, you must provide a united front for your rebellious child and for any other children you have in your home.

Through our time with Ryan, we realized how important it is to recognize that husbands and wives don't arrive at the same time on the journey through grief and pain. People respond at different rates and with different intensities to the issues and problems that arise in a home with a rebellious child. The worst thing for every member of the family—including the rebellious child—is to see Mom and Dad disagreeing about how to handle problems caused by that child.

I'm not a proponent of parents always taking their disagreements behind closed doors. If you do, your children never see conflict resolution modeled in a healthy way. However, if you and your spouse are vehemently opposed to one another's approach on how to deal with or respond to the actions, words, or results of a rebellious child, then I suggest taking the argument behind closed doors. You must respectfully remove yourselves from the presence of your kids and prayerfully work out a relief plan.

You must also guard against infiltration of indifference to one another during these tough times. Ann and I continued in counseling with Ryan even after he left home. We realized how great a threat this circumstance could be to our marriage. You're going to be so tired that your biggest task might be to get out of bed in the morning. You're going to be so talked out that a two syllable word will be a triumph. You may be so emotionally drained that you feel about as romantic as a slug.

Again, I'll be blunt: When you are in the midst of a situation like this, guard your marriage. Tend to the needs of your spouse. Make intentional appointments to spend time together where communication and intimacy can flow freely and naturally. If you are not intentional, your marriage will suffer—and just might be destroyed.

Maintain Integrity with Your Other Children

Part of "keeping up the farm" is making sure your other children are not neglected. For example, when we first began experiencing difficulty with Ryan, we spent hours and hours talking with him, reasoning with him, praying for him, encouraging him to do what was right. Of course, this was good. But after months and months of spending nearly every night with Ryan, we noticed that our four other kids—the ones who were respectful, obedient, and reciprocal—were starting to get fed up with parents who spent all their time with the one who was hurting, disobeying, and defying them the most. Kids aren't stupid. Sometimes intentionally and sometimes unintentionally, they'll react to the situation and they will act out.

And after Ryan had run off a time or two and then dropped back in, we became incensed with his disregard for his two teenage sisters who loved him dearly, and we became intolerant of his selfish disregard for the emotions of his five- and six-year-old little brother and sister who nearly idolized him.

After a period of time, Ann and I came to the difficult decision together—again with proper biblical counsel—that we had to deliver an ultimatum to Ryan. He had to straighten up and live as a responsible part of our household, or we would put him in a group home. We let him know how much we loved him and we wanted him in our home, but we couldn't allow that in his current state. We made the decision that we were not going to sacrifice the other four kids on the altar of Ryan's rebellion.

That was probably the toughest decision we've ever made. But regardless of the consequences, intimidations, or threats, we had to protect our home. We decided that we needed to maintain our home so that when Ryan was ready to return, a home would actually be waiting for him. If you have a rebellious child, you must calculate the cost on the rest of the family, and after prayer and biblical counseling, you must take whatever steps are necessary to preserve your home and your integrity with your other children.

Maintain Integrity with Yourself

What do I mean? I'm talking about the private thoughts of hatred and bitterness, of retaliation and revenge you harbor toward your rebellious child and anyone who you perceive to have caused his rebellion. I never realized how creative I could be until I began to plot and scheme in my mind about what I could do to the person who I thought had stolen my son's innocence.

You have to be careful about maintaining your integrity personally or you'll become a victim of what you hate. You'll become something you don't like very much. You'll want so badly to save your child from whatever self-destructive path he has chosen that you'll fall into the trap of thinking that you can change his mind or that you can control him.

Probably the most difficult lesson Ann and I learned is the one that has given us the greatest relief. It has given us the greatest sense of peace, and the ability to pick up with our lives and go on: We finally realized that we can't solve Ryan's problem.

You Can't Solve Your Child's Problems

Unless something is chemically or physically wrong with your child, you can't solve his problem. His rebellion isn't against you. It's against God.

Ann and I tried to do everything for Ryan. We tried

to rescue him from his self-destructive path—which is what we should try to do as parents. But there came a point when we realized we couldn't rescue him. You can't evade the consequences of the choices rebellious children make.

Probably the toughest thing to do is to allow your child to experience the pain of his wrong choices. We have this natural inclination to prevent our children from getting hurt. The only problem is that when we try to short-circuit the natural consequences, we only prolong the hurt, not prevent it. The question becomes: Do we let them suffer the consequences now, or later on down the road when they become more entrenched in their rebellion, more entangled in their lifestyle?

We often pray for our kids to break free of the wrong crowd or the wrong influences. But then when God begins to move in our kids' lives—perhaps in ways that we don't particularly like, we get in the way of God's course of correction.

Parents have to get out of the way and let pain do its job. Your child has made a choice that ultimately involves him and God. Your child has to get right with God. When that happens, then the horizontal relationships—over time and with guidance—can get in line. Ann and I realized we were sometimes trying to do a job only God can do along with Ryan. You have to come to grips with the fact that you can't solve your child's problem. Relieve yourself of that pressure.

Don't Give Up

There's a difference between giving your child and his problems over to God and giving up. You give the situation to God because there is really not a whole lot you can do about it anyway. Jesus Christ is the head of the search-and-rescue team for rebellious teens and he does a tremendous job of it. Give it over to him, but don't give up.

Parents who are hurting, take your stand and keep it and you don't try to intercept your children as they are crashing. But when they are ready to change, when they are ready to end their trek of self-destruction, when they are ready to engage you and your family in a healthy, positive way—then you *must* be there to assist them make those changes.

Chapter 11

Friends and Family

I guess most parents would agree that our kids can be our greatest source of pleasure in life. And they can be our greatest source of pain. How about when your kids grow up and start to leave home? What kind of relationship will you have? I marvel when I talk to men who refer to the close "friendship" they have with their adult sons, or the women who talk about their adult daughters being their closest friends.

How can family members become friends? That's an odd question if you have younger children, because we tend to always see our children just as children. But as our kids grow older, they move from dependence toward independence. As they mature, do they understand their need to move to interdependence? Interdependence is the natural third step, but it can be just as hard as any other stage of a parent-child relationship. If you're at this stage—your child is now an adult and seems to be ready to become your friend—how can you help it occur?

Three Ways Family Becomes Friends

Of course, like all of parenting, there's no clear age when parents and children should move from one stage to the next. In fact, parenting is a lot about preparation. Even as you and your children move through one stage, you're preparing for the following stages. What you do in the present stage affects what happens in the next stage. So, the following ideas aren't as much what happens when your children are adults as they are ideas to prepare them for their adult relationship with you.

Sharing Experiences

Early on, you need to recognize how life's everyday experiences turn into bonding sessions. It starts as early as the crib. Don't wait until your children get to be a certain age before you start to share experiences with them. Some parents use the excuse, "Oh, they're too young to understand the significance of that."

Start early. A good place to start is bedtime. Finishing strong is important in every avenue of life, and finishing a day strong for our children is vital. Spending time with your children, tucking them in, praying with them before they go to sleep are all golden opportunities for bonding with our children.

Have your kids ever started crying out for you in the

middle of the night because they were scared or had a nightmare from a scary show or story they read? Maybe you remember the terror of the nightmares you experienced as a child. Your mind doesn't stop working at night. The mind is an amazing thing—it can cram for a test and still assimilate all that information and reproduce it, sometimes with greater clarity, after sleep. Thoughts, ideas, hopes, and values that are placed in the mind before bed tend to marinate during sleep in much the same way.

The final thoughts of your children's day can either be the last TV show you let them watch, their homework, or they can be thoughts you soften their pillow with. You can pray with them and teach them about God and his love for them. By doing this, you continue to develop that spiritual foundation in their lives. You can remind them of how much you love them. You can reaffirm their value. You can make the final picture of their day give them the peaceful rest they need and energize them for their tomorrow. Turn nighttime into a bonding experience. Wind down the day with sessions to solidify your relationships and give your children a jumpstart on tomorrow.

Lying down next to your children and reading them stories is great. My kids always preferred that I make up a story rather than read one. That takes creativity and energy, but it sticks in their minds. On several occasions, our youngest, Jordan, has said, "Daddy, will you tell me about Grumpy the Grasshopper? You remember." The truth is that I don't remember all the stories I've made up. But he sure can!

We've always tried to make reading from the Bible a natural part of this time. We use a great children's version with illustrations, and the kids stay transfixed on the pictures as we read to them. Teaching your children about God, his Word, and his love is the greatest gift and greatest shared experience you can give them. You don't have to be a Bible scholar or Sunday School teacher to do this. It's a valuable part of your responsibility to provide spiritual input and training for your children.

Shared experiences need to flow out of everyday happenings, and there also needs to be a time of planned shared experiences. As I've mentioned, some of the greatest, most enjoyable, and most memorable times can happen in an impromptu manner. But unless you plan to spend extended amounts of quantity time with your kids, the quality moments won't just happen.

Your shared experiences as a family just may become traditions. Family traditions are important in the process of seeing family members become friends. Traditions offer opportunities to create memories, to share love, and to build strong bonds between family members. A family tradition is a positive "habit" that is both anticipated and remembered. Good traditions inspire loyalty and unity and bring family members together. Through experience—almost without any of us even knowing it's happening—traditions help our children (and ourselves) understand and develop responsibility, values, sensitivity, communication, and individuality. (Go back to chapter 3 for more ways you can create bonding times as a family. Also, see the resources listed at the end of the book for additional ideas.)

We find ourselves living in a world that is less and less predictable, less and less dependable. We need to do all we can to ensure that our children feel like the family is a safe harbor in the storm—a place where warm and predictable things happen, where our children can develop identities of their own, where they can return (even if only in their memories), no matter how far from home they roam.

Jesus and his family understood the value of family traditions. Each year, they traveled with all their relatives and neighbors to Jerusalem. It was like a big family reunion road trip to celebrate Passover. One time, when they left Jerusalem to travel back home, Jesus' parents forgot him. They probably assumed he was with other family members. But it's an early version of the *Home Alone* story:

> Every year his parents went to Jerusalem for the Feast of the Passover. When he was twelve years old, they went up to the Feast, according to the custom. After the Feast was over, while his parents were returning home, the boy Jesus stayed behind in Jerusalem, but they were unaware of it. Thinking he was in their company, they traveled on for a day. Then they began looking for him among their relatives and friends. When they did not find him, they went back to Jerusalem to look for him.
>
> After three days they found him in the temple courts, sitting among the teachers,

> listening to them and asking them questions. Everyone who heard him was amazed at his understanding and his answers. When his parents saw him, they were astonished. His mother said to him, "Son, why have you treated us like this? Your father and I have been anxiously searching for you." (Luke 2:41-45)

I love this passage. It's one of my favorites in Scripture. Not just because it has spiritual significance to me, but because it's so real and down-to-earth. Jesus' parents struggled too. Ann and I have done the same thing—twice! Once in California and once in Chicago. We drove separate cars to church, and when we got home and took a head count, we were short a child!

It does my heart good to know that Jesus' earthly parents weren't perfect either. And after they messed up, they did the same thing any of us would do—they blamed their child!

Sharing in Adversity

When we decided to move from San Diego back to Chicago, it was a shock to our kids. We decided that to make the transition a little more palatable, we'd take a vacation on the way back to Chicago. Once the moving van packed up our household, we took off on our family vacation—two words which, according to Bill Cosby, are a contradiction in terms. Our trips across the country often seem to be versions of those *Vacation* movies with Chevy Chase!

Six hours into this trip, our van broke down eighteen miles outside of the hot metropolis of Gila Bend, Arizona. And I mean hot. It was a 118-degree day in July.

I had the van towed to Phoenix, while our four children and my pregnant wife stayed in the Stardust Motel in Gila Bend. The next morning I rented a car and picked up my family. We spent the day at a local water park and picked up our van that evening. An hour after picking it up, it started to stall out again. For the next three days, we chugged along all the way to Chicago, forced to skip all our planned vacation spots.

I can't remember how many times we've laughed about Gila Bend, Arizona since then. When we were going through it, we didn't laugh at all. But how many times have you gone on a vacation and though it was a disaster, later on you laughed about it? "Remember that time when Johnny was three and we went camping and he climbed in your sleeping bag and wet it? Oh, wasn't that hilarious?" "Remember when Mary threw up all over Tommy in the Tea Cups at Disneyland? Oh, what a killer!"

Some adversity doesn't allow you to look back and laugh. It makes you look back and say, "Whoa, thank God." Our frustrating trip from San Diego to Chicago ended up with us pulling into Chicago about an hour before closing on our house. After the closing we all went to the hotel restaurant. As my wife returned from the restroom I saw a look on her face that scared me in a way I'd never felt before. She summoned me over and told me that something was wrong. She was pregnant and she was afraid she'd lost the baby. After less than eight hours in this new town where we didn't know anyone or have any family, we landed in the emergency room. They performed an ultrasound and we had to wait until the next day for the results, but we were not given much hope that the baby had made it.

We had no one else, no friends or family in our new location. Only a hotel room and our family. That was a long night. A night of fear, of crying, of praying, of hoping. It was a night of questioning God and asking him "why" in some pretty serious language. It was a night of silence as we waited. These are the moments you don't go looking for, but when they come they bond you together like glue. The hospital visit the next day brought good news. Our baby was OK. He was a tough kid. And that turned out to be the case from the time Jordan was born until now. To give you an idea of his toughness, his nickname in our house during his toddler years was "Dr. Destructo"!

Good or bad, adversity builds bonding times. Of course, you're not going to go looking for trouble, but when it comes, the time shared can draw you closer together. The bonding doesn't necessarily take place in the midst of the crisis, but days, weeks, or months later you have a memory.

Sharing Faith

A national survey done by Nick Stinnet of the University of Nebraska studied hundreds of families characterized as "intimate families." The study reported six characteristics of a close family. One of the top six was a high degree of religious orientation. Families determined to be close or intimate held a common faith and participated in religious activities together.[1]

Many parents today are reacting to having religion crammed down their own throats. They respond with an attitude, "Well, I'm not going to cram religion down my kids' throats. I'm going to let them decide for themselves when they get old enough." We send an inaccurate message that moral and spiritual behavior and teaching is self-evident. Would you let your child watch any TV program, read any magazine, go to any movie, and let them decide for themselves whether or not it's appropriate? I don't think so.

In the same vein, why leave moral and spiritual teaching to default? It's the responsibility of parents. How do you do it? Teach your kids about God, about his love, and how to love him through shared life experiences.

Sharing faith means more than going to church on Christmas and Easter. Those are great, but that level of commitment is similar to eating meals only at Christmas and Easter. Sharing our faith with our kids comes through life experiences. Leaving them to default and chance would be remiss on your part as a parent.

What are some practical ways you can share your faith as a family?

1. Read a children's Bible together regularly.

The stories in these Bibles have great foundational truths and they can be understood by family members of all ages.

2. Establish one night a week as family night.

Use this time as a fun and creative way to build your family's faith together. Watch a video together and afterward discuss why certain characters in the story acted the way they did. Would they have responded to their situations differently if they had known God? (See the reference list for suggested materials.)

3. Pray with your kids regularly, not just at meals.

When your kids hear you speak directly and personally to God "because he's really there," then they begin to believe that God can hear us and does want to relate to us.

4. Find a strong church to become a part of as a family.

Become part of a church that is real and relevant. Make sure it has a solid children's program and youth group. It's a great asset to have church partner with you in your parenting.

These ways of sharing your faith are good, but they'll be useless unless you have personally established your relationship with God and are working on growing it.

Each of us needs to have a personal relationship with God. I'm not talking about "religion." I'm not talking about "ritual." Each one of us has to come to a point where we realize our need for this relationship. And God has made the provision for it! No religious hoops to jump through, no jargon to memorize or rattle off. The relationship comes simply by asking and receiving His provision—His Son—into your life.

As a parent I've made mistakes, but as a person I've done even worse. I've done probably the same kinds of things you have. I've lied, cheated, blown my top, hurt people, let God down—sound familiar? These things separate me from God, but his provision pays the penalty for all those things. I just need to receive God's provision, his gift, his Son. That's all there is to establishing a relationship with God.

Once you've done that, you'll want to grow in that relationship and understand how you can incorporate his wisdom and power into your life. Just like any relationship, it needs to grow and be nurtured. Communication needs to be developed to allow your relationship with God to flourish. Find a readable version of the Bible and begin to talk with him about what you've read. Plug into a good church—one that makes sense, that is relevant, and that truly respects God's Word.

Your life, your involvement as a parent is critical to your family's growing and sharing a faith that really makes a difference. Parental involvement is necessary for passing on moral and spiritual teaching. Make God a natural topic of conversation. Tell your children and let them see it when God is working in your life.

Our family had an experience nine years ago that I think sums up this chapter's thoughts. We took our family back to my parents' in Iowa for a family reunion. It's always fun to see my brothers and their families. Now—

no offense intended—Iowa would not be my choice for vacation if it weren't for my family. Sorry, Hawkeyes. It gets pretty hot and muggy during Midwest summers. But the fun and relief we find from the weather is to head out on the lake and water-ski all day long.

Through the years, I've taught all my kids to ski. On this particular trip, we headed out to the lake and had been skiing all morning. We took a lunch break, then headed back into the boat for the afternoon round. My brother was in the back "spotting" for me as I drove the boat. My daughter, April, didn't want to ski, so she climbed into the front of the boat. As we were getting the next skier ready in the water, I had to throw the rope—a competition slalom ski rope with a metal handle covered with rubber—out to the skier. I stood up in the middle of the boat, yelled "heads down" as usual, and started swinging the rope rapidly in a circle above my head like Roy Rogers. All of a sudden the rope stopped in midswing. I looked around to see that April had stood up in the front of the boat and started walking to the back. As I swung the rope with tremendous force, the ski handle struck her in the head. She fell limp and the blood poured.

I knew exactly what had happened. As I held her in my arms, my brother drove the boat to the shore. I carried April to the car and then my wife held her in the backseat. We were way out in the country with no phones. I sped into town, running red lights, passing on the shoulder, driving like a crazy man until I reached the closest hospital. April still laid motionless in my wife's lap.

At the hospital, April went into convulsions. They transferred her by ambulance to a hospital specializing in children. Within a half hour, she was in emergency neurosurgery. We didn't know if she was going to come out of surgery alive. Within an hour, the hospital waiting room was packed with brothers, sisters-in-law, parents, and friends. I don't know when I've felt more like dying in my own life. I thought that I'd killed my little girl and I'd rather die myself. And as my brothers and parents surrounded me, their wives went into another room to pray. I forced myself to call Ann's parents in California and tell them. Her dad comforted me and attempted to lighten my load with his words.

April came out of surgery—with half her head shaved and looking like she'd gone 15 rounds. She'd lost all her speech, but she had gained her life back. For the next nine days, Ann and I slept next to her in her hospital room as my family continued to pour out their support, prayers, and love.

April recovered nicely and had to learn to talk all over again. I can assure you (from looking at my phone bill) that she recovered quite well. She's now in college and doing great. But I don't know how we would have made it through that horrible time without the love, friendship, and support our extended family offered.

1. Nick Stinnett with John DeFrain, *Seeds of Strong Families*, 1st edition (Boston: Little, Brown, © 1985), introduction.

Chapter 12

Your Family's Future

When our third teenager got her driver's permit, I started thinking about when I was sixteen. It wasn't so easy to get a license back then. When I was ready to take my driving test, my dad gave me the line you might have heard: "Now, Son, driving's not a right, it's a responsibility." Sound familiar? To make sure I understood the responsibility part, my dad decided to set some parameters.

I remember the three conditions my dad required I meet before I could get my license: (1) I had to get my grades up; (2) I had to read my Bible every day; and (3) I had to get my hair cut.

So when I got my report card I raced to my dad and said, "Here it is! Nothing below a B!" He said I was one-third of the way there, and then asked me about my Bible reading. I reported that I was reading it each day.

Then he questioned me about his third condition. "How about that haircut?" he asked. I told him I'd been reading in the Bible about Jesus, and how in all the illustrations artists have done picturing him, he had long hair. My dad responded, "Yeah, and he walked everywhere, didn't he?"

Now for the truth: My dad never said that, and my report card was never B's and above, I didn't read my Bible every day, and I definitely didn't get my hair cut. But as parents, we like to control things, and we do like to issue the orders in our families.

In this book, we've talked a lot about control, choices, and circumstances. Effective parenting is determined to a great degree by our ability to negotiate control in our kids' lives. What should we control? What should we let happen by chance? When our kids are young, a great deal of control is necessary. But as they grow older and we still want to control them, we can't! The stage is set for our future family based on how we deal with control.

As you consider the future of your family, three explosive issues need to be addressed. These may feel like "minefields." And dealing with them won't be easy. But how you understand these areas will make a significant impact on the health of your family in the future.

As you read this chapter, some of the information will feel like review. Some of it is. Other sections will seem like a summary of other things I've said. It is. And some of it is new too. Consider all of it my parting shot at helping you take off on the spiritual side of parenting.

Leaving and Cleaving

The first couple chapters of the Bible record God's creation of the world and lay the groundwork for all humanity. God created the heavens and the earth and pronounced them "good." He created the skies, water, and animals and said, "It is good."

Then God created man, and what did he say? "It's not good for man to be alone." So he created woman. Then the two of them came together and God instructed them that when they had children, those children would have to one day leave the family and cleave to their spouses.

When children become adults, there must come a time when there is a redefinition of the family dynamic. As they grow they have to learn to *individuate* themselves from their families of origin. They become individuals. There will come a time when you will need to learn to release your kids, to help them head out into this world to raise their own families.

This principle of "leave and cleave" needs to happen in your family. If you don't understand the different ways you have to relate to your children at different stages in their lives, you can expect some destructive forces in your families. Three different pictures describe our developing relationships with family members.

Leg-Grabbing Stage

The first stage is symbolized by a toddler who sneaks up and grabs your leg. He may not be able to see your face but he grabs your leg for a sense of security and direction. You can even try walking around pulling that kid along on your leg. You take responsibility for them in almost every area of their lives.

But your goal in this caregiver stage when the kid is wrapped around your thigh is to teach him how to begin to fend for himself in a not-so-friendly world. You do your best to teach him about right and wrong, about his significance to you, and most importantly, how significant he is to his Father in heaven.

Shirt-Button Stage

As I grew older I used to hug my mom around the waist. She would measure me as I grew according to her shirt buttons. It's a different stage. Kids still look up to you and need direction. They want you to assure them of their significance and security. But along the way they want to assume more responsibility for their own lives.

And that's your goal at this stage. Just as they naturally pull away from you a little more often when you hug them—especially in front of their friends—you need to allow them to pull away. They earn responsibility by demonstrating to you that they can handle responsibility. You give a little and they earn more. If they disappoint you and blow it, you pull back for a while until they earn that level of responsibility back.

Eye-to-Eye Stage

Eventually, your children look you in the eyes. Believe it or not, this is often the most difficult stage for parents. The adult-to-adult relationship is based on trust, love, and respect. Again, it's a gradual process that doesn't happen overnight.

You wouldn't dream of giving your twelve-year-old the keys to the car, shoving the classifieds in his hand, and saying, "Go find an apartment!" These steps of release need to be moved through gradually. But if the process of individuation doesn't happen, if you don't allow your children to become adult children, all kinds of damage can occur. On the other hand, children who refuse to grow up and accept responsibility will experience great trouble in their lives.

Children who grow up without being allowed to accept responsibility will likely have many problems in their lives such as: inordinate need for approval from others; lack of autonomy and self-confidence; chronic fear of failure; all good or all bad perception of life and people; extreme anxiety around authority figures; unhealthy dependencies on others; depression; sexual inhibitions; repression; and confusion.

I have seen these symptoms displayed many times. It's especially hurtful when it happens to one of your friends. A friend I've known for fifteen years went into graduate school with me. When we first got to know each other I was really impressed by his relationship with his father. He called him all the time. He told me about their conversations.

But as I began to observe this relationship more closely, I saw that my friend was making major life decisions, then changing direction midcourse. Whether about his graduate studies, career choices, or relationships, I'd notice how his mind would fluctuate after phone conversations with his dad. This was especially evident when he began to get close to a woman. Each woman he dated became "a tool of Satan," according to his father. He couldn't even enter into a healthy relationship or make a major life decision without his dad forcing him to do a "180."

His dad would quote verses to him like "children, obey your parents" and "honor your father and your mother." Because he wanted to honor his parents, my friend wouldn't follow through on many of his major life decisions. As friends and counselors confronted him, he began to take some tough steps toward individuation. His parents fought him every step of the way. They ostracized him, called him names. I was a groomsman in his wedding, and his parents weren't there. In fact, my friend had to hire a security guard to stand watch outside, because his father had threatened to storm the church.

Fortunately, my friend began to understand these stages and took tough steps to work through them. As children we need to obey our parents. But moving into a relationship of honoring doesn't demand that we follow everything our parents say as we become adult children. We must develop our own understanding of right and wrong and accept responsibility for our own decisions.

Over time, a maturing child has to give himself permission to move away from leg grabbing and shirt buttons to move up to that eye-to-eye position. He needs to take responsibility for his own thoughts, feelings, and decisions. Growing children begin to feel more freedom to disagree with their parents and to stick to their own perceptions and convictions. Again, there are no magical ages when these steps happen for different children. It's as your children begin to live responsibly that you give them more responsibility. And you give them a lot of grace when it comes to how they live out their individuation, remembering that you can't protect them from every potential evil they might encounter.

As children grow, they have to develop realistic pictures of their parents. This is tough on kids! I remember as a twenty-year-old toiling with this. I loved my parents so much and I wanted them to be perfect. I'd always believed they were perfect! In the back of my mind, I knew it wasn't really true. But it was an illusion I wanted to hang onto. Some of us have a difficult time accepting that our parents are human.

This developmental process is God's design. Both the maturing child and the parents have to acknowledge this if they are to develop and maintain healthy relationships. If you have adolescents, you need to be on your knees asking God for wisdom in the control/release process. And if your children are already grown, you need to back away and give them room.

When your children move through these stages, you'll discover some wonderful things in your relationships. When you come to this point of respecting your adult children, your family can stay close for years without all the fighting and other garbage that kills many families. When you follow God's designs for relationships, you'll reap benefits you'll never regret. But let's be completely honest—it's a tough process.

Processing Our Pain

One of my favorite stories is about a little boy who asks his mom, "Where did I come from?"

His mom answers with the story about the stork.

So he asks, "Well, Mommy, where did you come from?"

She answers that she came from the stork as well.

Not satisfied with these answers, the boy talks to his grandma. When she answers with another rendition of the stork story, the boy finally gives up and goes outside to play with his friends.

"You know what?" he tells them. "There hasn't been a normal birth in this family for three generations!"

Maybe you had a normal birth. But chances are that you didn't have a normal upbringing—whatever that is! Most of us carry pain from the past generation or two into our own parenting.

If I could attach a meter to measure your reaction when you think about pain from your past, it might move all over the place! If you had a painful childhood, you might be thinking you can never overcome the trauma.

Of course, the feeling is made worse by well-intentioned people who advise, "Don't worry about the pain of your past! Just give it over to Jesus. He'll sprinkle some magical dust on it and it will all be gone." On the other end of the spectrum are those who say, "You'll need at least ten years of intensive therapy. If your mom didn't change your diapers enough, you'll need at least ten years to sort it all out!"

I don't want to make light of the significant troubles you might have faced as a child. And I certainly don't want to minimize the healing power of Jesus. But if you're honest, you'll admit that how you were raised affects the way you think and the way you relate. It affects the way you understand your spouse, your children, your neighbors, your extended family—even your in-laws!

How has the pain of my past affected me today? A critical question I often ask myself is, "How will the mistakes I make in raising my five kids affect them? How will this play out in their lives?" Ouch! Want more pain? Check out Numbers 14:18:

> The Lord is slow to anger, abounding in love and forgiving sin and rebellion. Yet he does not leave the guilty unpunished; he punishes the children for the sin of the fathers to the third and fourth generation.

The sins and the mistakes parents make do affect children. You don't need a research analyst or a psychologist to see how some of the most appalling social behaviors we see in individuals happen because of the horrendous upbringing in their families.

Look at two contemporary rock stars. Read the lyrics of Eddie Vedder, lead singer of Pearl Jam. You'll quickly recognize the ugliness in his relationship with his father and the pain he endured because of his divorced parents. You get the sense that writing and singing about it is somehow his way to process that pain.

There's another lead singer who didn't process it as well. When you read about Nirvana's Kurt Cobain and his childhood—his abandonment to the point where he even lived as a homeless man under a bridge—you sense the depth of his pain. But you also must believe there was a better way to process that pain than taking a shotgun and blowing himself away.

Too many parents today grew up being "lateraled" like a football, tossed back and forth between Mom and Dad. And even if your parents stayed together, were you ever told something like, "You're never going to be what your brothers were" or "You're never going to be as smart as your sisters"? How about "That B should have been an A" or "You could have scored 15 points per game instead of 10" or "You should have been elected class president instead of vice president"? A lot of us are charter members of the "never enough" club. Your whole life pattern is one of equating performance with love.

Whether your own family dysfunction was at this level or a more severe one, you can't simply sweep these issues under the rug. They'll have an impact on you, on your parenting, and on your children's children in the years to come.

Ann and I spent some time counseling a friend of ours. We confronted this married woman about her tendency to enter relationships with older men. Her parents were divorced and her father had abandoned her.

She really wanted to have a strong relationship with a father figure. She ended up being raped by one older man, having an affair with another, and was ready to cash in her marriage. Her self-esteem and sense of security were severely marred. Do you think she needed to give attention to this pain from her past?

We can't ignore what's going on—not around us—but right in our close circle of relationships. Millions of adults are now grown-up victims of all kinds of child abuse. It is estimated that 19 percent of all American women and 9 percent of all men were sexually abused as children.[1] Another study shows that as many as 1.5 million American children may be suffering from either emotional, physical, or sexual abuse.[2] If there was abuse of any kind in your family growing up, you owe it to yourself and to those you love to "get at" the issues and begin to work through the pain.

Some people feel so badly damaged they don't feel equipped to deal with the complexities of all this. It's courageous to admit that you don't have the tools and you need to seek help. Again, it's a tough step. But I want to encourage you that seeking help is not a sign of weakness. It's a mark of strength. At different difficult seasons of my life, I've spent time in counseling. I wanted to understand how to negotiate difficult issues in my own parenting.

Be honest with yourself. Speak the truth to yourself. Think about how you're going to process whatever pain you're feeling so you can be free—free to relate to God in an authentic way and to others who are important to you.

Caring for My Aging Parents

A final issue related to the future of our families is how we relate to the elderly. In case you think this shouldn't warrant much space in this book, consider this: *US News and World Report* says the fastest growing age segment in the United States is the sixty-five and older age-group.[3] As a group, middle-aged people now have more parents than they do children. More than one half of the people in the over sixty-five age-group will require long-term care in a facility. And 90 percent of those entering a nursing home will be bankrupt within two years if they must pay their own expenses.[4]

God says when you honor your parents he will pour blessing into your life. Paul gives us a strong exhortation in 1 Timothy:

> Give proper recognition to those widows who are really in need. But if a widow has children or grandchildren, these should learn first of all to put their religion into practice by caring for their own family and so repaying their parents and grandparents, for this is pleasing to God. (1 Timothy 5:3-4)

Could Scripture be much clearer? If you have aging parents, it's your responsibility to care for them. I recognize this issue is complex and can easily be misunderstood. I'm not advising children never to put their parents into care facilities. But use common sense. Use biblical instruction. Be sensitive to your aging parents.

Be willing to make sacrifices to care for your parents. And don't fall prey to the trap of taking the path of convenience.

When I was a freshman in high school, my grandmother came to live with us for a few months at a time. On one of her visits, she fell and broke her hip and was hospitalized for almost a year. I saw my mother drive to the hospital every day to visit her. And when she was released, we brought her home and she lived with us for the next five years.

As a family, we learned what it meant to take care of Grandma. Caregiving involved so much more than the fun times of sitting around telling stories. It meant feeding and bathing her. It meant getting her out of bed and helping her to the bathroom. As a high schooler, I watched my grandmother suffer the shame and humiliation of not being able to care for herself. Yet along the way, I also learned from my mom and dad what it meant to really care for a person and help that person maintain a sense of dignity.

Honoring doesn't stop when you leave and cleave. We are always to honor our parents. This is God's way to provide care. A great illustration comes from the life of Christ. When Jesus was hanging on the cross, dying for my sins and yours with the weight of redemption on him, he looked down and saw his mother. He singled out his closest friend, the Apostle John, and asked him to take care of his mother. Jesus had a lot on his mind, a lot on his heart, a lot of stress and pain hanging on the cross, but he made sure he entrusted his mother to the most compassionate human being he knew.

I strongly believe that the future of our family depends on how we deal with the issues of leaving and cleaving, of processing our pain, and of caring for our aging parents. Will you be willing to make some tough choices to ensure the long-range health of your family?

When the late Senator Paul Tsongas contemplated running for President a few years ago, he shocked the country with an announcement. He'd been a self-proclaimed workaholic. He lived for the Washington beltway scene. Then one day he discovered that he had cancer. He left Washington and went home to do some soul-searching. His statement made a profound impact on me. He said, "When I get to the end of my life and I'm lying on my deathbed, I don't think I'll say, 'Gee, I wish I had spent more time at the office.'"[5]

The future of your family depends on what kind of deposit you're willing to make in them during your lifetime.

1. Russel Watson with Gerald Lubenow, Nikkifinke Greenberg, Patricia King, Darby Junkin, "A Hidden Epidemic," *Newsweek*, May 14, 1984, 30–36.

2. Margaret M. Heckler, "Introduction," *Perspectives in Child Maltreatment* (U.S. Department of Health and Human Services, National Center on Child Abuse and Neglect, n.d.), 1.

3. David Gergen. (1990) "Sixtysomething," *US News and World Report*, April 16, 64.

4. Dr. Stanley Cath (1983) "If You Have to Care for Your Aging Parent," *US News and World Report,* Oct. 3, 75.

5. James S. Heweth, ed. *Illustrations Unlimited* (Wheaton, Ill., Tyndale House Publishing, June 1998).

RESOURCES

- "Right Track" Tapes by Ron Clarkson. P.O. Box 62756, Colorado Springs, CO 80962 or call (719) 531-6900

Fun/Activity Books

- *Family Nights Tool Chest Series*, by Jim Weidmann and Kurt Bruner, Victor, 1997, 1998
- *Big Book of Family Fun*, by Claudia Arp and Linda Dillow, Nelson, 1994
- *Fun Things to Do with Your Child*, by Carl Dreizler and Phil Phillips, Galahad Books, 1995
- *Together at Home*, by Dean and Grace Merrill, Tyndale, 1996
- *Families That Play Together Stay Together*, by Cameron and Donna Partow, Bethany House, 1996

Parent Strengthening/Encouraging Books

- *How to Really Love Your Child*, by Ross Campbell, Victor, 1992
- *Guilt-Free Parenting*, by Robert and Debra Bruce and Ellen W. Oldacre, Dimensions for Living, 1997

- *The Heritage*, by J. Otis Ledbetter and Kurt Bruner, Victor, 1996
- *What Every Mom Needs*, by Elisa Morgan and Carol Kuykendall, Zondervan, 1995
- *The Family Fragrance*, by J. Otis Ledbetter and Gail Ledbetter, Victor, 1998
- *How to Really Love Your Teenager*, by Ross Campbell, Victor, 1993

Relationship-Building Books

- *The Marriage You've Always Wanted*, Ron Lee, editor, Victor, 1997
- *Now We're Talking*, by Robert C. Crosby, Focus on the Family, 1996
- *When Prince Charming Falls Off His Horse*, by Jerry and Judy Schreur, Victor, 1997
- *Where the Wild Strawberries Grow*, by David and Claudia Arp, Victor, 1996
- *365 Ways to Build Your Child's Self-Esteem*, by Cheri Fuller, Pinon Press, 1994
- *52 Simple Ways to Build Your Child's Self-Esteem and Confidence*, by Jan Dagartz, Nelson,

1991

- *Fathers and Sons* and *Fathers and Daughters*, by Jack and Jerry Schreur, Victor, 1995
- *The Gift of the Blessing*, by Gary Smalley and John Trent, Nelson, 1993
- *Fun Excuses to Talk about God*, by Joani Schultz, Group Publishing, 1997

Parenting Advice

- *The Media-Wise Family*, by Ted Baehr, Victor, 1998
- *Front Porch Parenting*, by Mary Manz Simon, Victor, 1997

Counseling/Helps

- *Families Where Grace Is in Place*, by Jeff Van Vonderan, Bethany House, 1992
- *Parenting Passages*, by David R. Veerman, Tyndale, 1995
- *The Attention Deficit Child*, by Grant Martin, Victor, 1998

- *Raising Emotionally Healthy Kids*, by H. Norman Wright and Gary J. Oliver, Victor, 1995

Faith/Spiritual Training Resources

- *The Family Book of Christian Values*, by Stuart and Jill Briscoe, Victor, 1995

- *365 Ways to Develop Your Child's Values*, by Cheri Fuller, Pinon Press, 1994

- *Talks to Boys and Talks to Girls*, by Eleanor A. Hunter, NavPress, 1996

- *Helping Children Know God*, by various authors, Group Publishing, 1995

- *Building a Foundation for Your Child's Faith*, by Larry D. Stephens, Zondervan, 1996

If you liked this book,
check out these great titles from
ChariotVICTOR Publishing . . .

This book is for those looking for a thoughtful, common-sense approach to building a stable, loving foundation for their families. It demonstrates how to strengthen your heritage by understanding the roots you're given, and it shows you how to chart a new course by leaving behind the negative aspects of your family inheritance. Sprinkled throughout are insightful and inspiring stories of the authors' own family experiences.

The Heritage
by J. Otis Ledbetter & Kurt Bruner
ISBN: 1-56476-694-2

In today's society, there is little time left for families to come together and experience their spiritual heritage. "Family night" was designed to help parents intentionally set aside a time when their heritage could be passed along. Fun, short, and powerful, this alternative to family devotions makes "Bible time" enjoyable for all ages. This is the fourth title in the Family Night Tool Chest series and contains 12 sessions to help parents create a time of spiritual growth for their children.

Family Night Tool Chest
Wisdom Life Skills
by Jim Weidmann & Kurt Bruner
ISBN: 0-78143-015-1